GENESIS:

The Bullet Was Meant For Me – D.C. Sniper Story Untold

By
Isa Farrington-Nichols

Eloquent Books
New York, New York

Eloquent Books
An imprint of AEG Publishing Group
845 Third Avenue, 6th Floor - 6016
New York, NY 10022
www.eloquentbooks.com

ISBN 978-1-09834-207-4

Printed in the United States of America

Book Design: Linda W. Rigsbee

Disclaimer

This book is a non-fiction account and true story of my life and the tragic events that lead to the murder of my niece ,Keenya Cook, in my Tacoma, Washington home. It is a true story of my life and the relationship that I had with convicted D.C. sniper, John Allen Muhammad. It is a true story of my friendship with his ex-wife Mildred Muhammad and her family. This book is a stimulus to a road of self-discovery. It is not the intention of this book to judge, condemn, or ridicule anyone in any way. It is an account of the first murder that precipitated the murders on the East Coast known as the DC Sniper Shootings. It is a balm to the many that are hurting, and disenfranchised.

To Mom's Babies; Tasherra Louise Farrington-Marshall, my son-in-law Allen Marshall, and Tamara Jean Farrington-Nichols
To Big Mamma's Grand Babies; Alleera Leah Marshall, Tameera Marie Marshall, And Akeera Lynnell Marshall,
To my immediate family; my mother, Louise Farrington (deceased); my father, James Farrington; my brothers, Joseph and Rockwell; and my sisters, Sheila and Lynnel (deceased).
Thank you for your prayers and unconditional love as I found the way back to the Genesis of family.
You bring me much joy!

Acknowledgements

Our Father who art in Heaven, hallowed be thy name. Thy Kingdom come, thy will be done, on Earth as it is in Heaven.... Father bless the hearers of these words. Bless those who read these pages. LORD, allow your love to conquer and restore those you have put into my life that chose to do me evil. Father, I thank you for the many people that you have sent to me and the many people whom you knew I would need in my life. I thank you for having someone there to help me bear the loads. In my darkest, loneliest hour, you placed someone there. Thank you for your love that destroys the yokes of bondage, abandonment, resentment, and pain. Thank you for your love that lifted your son Jesus. Your love has lifted me!

There are not enough pages to thank everyone for loving me. But, I will try. Thanks to my family....those living in San Diego like Jacqueline (Jakki), Debbie, Ajamu and Tamara, James, Sherrie, Asonja , Caleb, Melyssa, Joshua, Jacob, Shahra, Brittani, Elbertha Burks, Phyllis, Myra (Doll), Fredrick, Harold and Donna Carter, Marcella, Karen (KK), Donna (Dee), Vicky, Terrance and Enako. Thank you to my Uncle Willie and Aunt Ella in Texas, and Aunt Mary and Uncle Will in Alabama.

Thank you to my Northwest folks... Apostles Stan and Renee Taylor, Scherita and Schreeya Taylor, Linda Braddy, Dr. Ruth Barnes, Prophetess Kim White, Missionary Melannie Melvin-Brown, Cherylynn Cobb, Michael and Juanita Twiggs, Jim and Gail Merritt-Smith, Dr. Darya Funches, Ted and Billie Johnstone, John "JJ" Jones, Dr. Charles Horne of PacRim, Attorney Gerald Burke, Thomas Dixon, Valerie Yarborough, Tony and Lorraine Hudson, Ebben and Cheryl Jones, Cecil Stewman, Stephen Whitmore, Melannie Cunningham, Robert Henly Jr., Pamela Martinez, Frankie Elzie, Earl and Anya Wright, Keith and Andreta Armstrong, Michael Belcher, Tony and Barbara Wright, Mary Caldwell (Ms East), and Pastors Donald and Kathy Shorter.

A special thank you to Eba for the Genesis, you were scribing in the beginning; Larry in Raleigh for the beginning audio, you were so patient with "TT;" John "JJ" Jones, Karen "KK" Howard, and Valerie for your time and hours of editing; Tony and Barbara Wright in England, for if it had not been for your generous English airline ticket to stop my hemorrhaging; Shyan Selah/BNW Entertainment, the melodies from the beginning of Keenya will keep her memory alive; and Dr. Maxine Buie Mimms and your "house of healing."

A man who has friends must himself be friendly. But there is a friend who sticks closer than a brother. Proverbs 18:2

Table Of Contents

Preface

Prophetic Word & Testimony

Oh daughter, You are so dear to Me.

For I have heard your plea; I, Shaddai, the Almighty.

I have listened to you, now listen to ME. For I am calling you into your destiny!

I have a call on your life; yes indeed, it has been there since you were in the womb you see. I have a call on your life, everything is okay. Fear not, for I am with you always.

Not just a wife, mother, daughter, sister, friend; I have created you to be a woman of God, its time to begin. Abide in Me as I abide in you. I will lead you through. I will continue to bless you exceedingly, abundantly indeed, for these things I promised, so continue to obey Me! Look to the hills from whence cometh your help, there you will always find Me.

It is not my desire to let the locust and the canker worm steal your joy for I am El Roi, the God who sees, the responder to needs. Sow a seed if you do not believe, I will pour you out a blessing, you will not have room enough to receive.

Oh daughter, I hear your plea, praying for wisdom in what looks like a catastrophe. Do not try to change him, leave him to Me. I am the only one that can heal, deliver, and set free. You are the mother of a child or more, a blessed one indeed. Let them see how fearfully and wonderfully I made thee.

Oh daughter of Zion, you are safe with Me. For I dwell in a secret place in the Most High. I am a refuge and a fortress, put your trust in Me. I come to give you life, life more abundantly. It is My love for you that I talk to you this way. You were bought with a price. It has already been paid.

It was for love I gave My blood.

It was through My blood that you are saved and loved!
Isa Farrington-Nichols
January 22, 2002

Genesis: The DC Sniper Story Untold

Foreword by Darya Funches, Ed.D.

In 2002, the lives of over 21 people and their families crossed through the actions of the DC Snipers, making a permanent mark in the minds and hearts of a nation. Isa Farrington-Nichols' revealing book, *Genesis*, speaks about the first in the series of seemingly random murders, for which she was the intended victim. After being silent for five years, her story brings to our attention a web of events behind the scenes. We learn that her niece, Keenya, was actually the first victim, mistaken for Nichols by the shooter. Isa Nichols' life and her family shattered.

To speak of the origins of the DC Snipers' reign of terror, Nichols has to speak of her relationship with the family of the mastermind sniper, John Muhammad. Most family members of the DC Snipers' victims cannot speak knowingly of a relationship with either of the snipers, John Muhammad or Lee Malvo. It seems that all the victims, including the first victim, Nichols' niece, were people who were in the wrong place at the wrong time, colliding with the deadly intentions of John Muhammad who made a promise to kill his estranged wife, Mildred, and her friend, Isa Nichols.

Genesis provokes us to learn from these murders and deaths if we are willing to examine our society and ourselves and take actions to heal, change, and create healthy families and responsible law enforcement in the face of domestic violence. Nichols' story grabs our attention, because it brings forth much of what was hidden about this series of murders that generated so much fear, terror, chaos, and grief across the nation. Almost without notice, she takes us on a journey from domestic differences, to domestic abuse, to domestic conflict, to domestic violence, to societal terror. Her story makes us realize that many of us may be touched by, or have stood in the face of domestic abuse without realizing it. Or if realizing it, have turned a blind eye. Her story wakes us up and tells us to take responsibility for recognizing the signals and to take action if we want to be a healthy society filled with healthy families.

As we read *Genesis*, we travel with Nichols in her account of her relationship with Mildred and John Muhammad and the parallel journey of her deteriorating relationship with her husband, Joseph Nichols. Looking closely, we begin to recognize that the untold story is more than the startling story about the first in the series of murders. It is about looking into consciousness of our society and ourselves. The untold story is about all of our histories with domestic abuse and violence, about our own unhealed wounds, and our hunger for unconditional love and acceptance. The untold story is also about the unseen ties between the murderers, those murdered and all of their families.

Domestic abuse and violence, which comes in many colors, are the threads woven between Nichols, her estranged husband, her niece, and her friends, the Muhammad Family. Domestic abuse and violence may also be threads woven in the lives of the law enforcement and the criminal justice system representatives who looked the other way when the women of this story sought protection and assistance. As readers of *Genesis*, we almost walk in Nichols' shoes as she exposes the delicate threads of emotions and thoughts that keep her in a distressed marriage and draw her to assist her friend, Mildred, in her distressed marriage in the years prior to Keenya's death in Tacoma and the explosion of deaths on the East Coast.

We can think of our own experiences with domestic harmony, abuse, and violence. We wonder about how our friendships and commitments to help others can place us at the center of a destructive tornado. We wonder whether this maelstrom could have been predicted and prevented, as each force and opposite force made their movements through the marriages and families of John and Mildred Muhammad and Joseph and Isa Nichols.

What are the magnets that draw together those who died and those who fired the mortal shots? Is it merely coincidence or being in the wrong place at the wrong time?

Or, were there deeper invisible connections that wove a web between victims and perpetrators of this violence? Do we learn to tolerate such treatment by watching how our fathers treat our mothers and how our mothers treat our fathers when we are young and absorbing future behaviors as we breathe the air around us? Such experiences can result in receiving, giving, and accepting abuse without even recognizing our parts in the phenomenon until some significant experience, like the death of a loved one, wakes us up. Isa Farrington-Nichols woke up.

Are our current law enforcement and criminal justice systems fertile soil to grow more perpetrators and victims of domestic violence, or can they prevent it? Is it because of the underlying beliefs and practices of these systems that we fail to prevent incidences of mortal violence, such as the series of DC Sniper killings? What has made our society so accepting and tolerant of domestic violence that we wait for murders to act?

Domestic violence is not always physical. It is spiritual. It is mental. It is emotional. It strikes in violations and betrayals of vows and agreements. It seeps through barrages of hurtful words, withdrawals, and criticisms, where one or both parties in the couple seek to kill the spirit of the other, bit by bit. The perpetrator looks through the site of his or her weapon, holding the target in view and perhaps injuring whoever stands nearby. The more we accept and tolerate such blows — whether under the auspice of our religions, our habits, our high levels of pain tolerance, our desperation to get love from those who are not offering what we want— the more we teach one another that these violations are acceptable ways to treat people that we supposedly love.

Yes, domestic violence is the thread connecting many of the people at the center of *Genesis*. Perhaps the unhealed wounds within each person compelled us into the story itself to experience the pain, grief, horror, and destruction of what happened before moving onto the learning, healing, insights, and renewal that can result. Only each person affected then and now can truly tell us.

As a first time author, Isa Farrington-Nichols has more than done her part in starting the conversation. She lets us into her shattered world with all of its pain, and then takes us to doorway of her own rebirth.

We are inspired as we read of her recovery and victory in life. We are comforted as she begins to love herself truly, no longer accepting less than she deserves in relationships. Our faith, hope, and love are renewed. Reading this book, we learn that the genesis, the first murder of the DC Sniper, was in Tacoma. We learn that the genesis was also domestic abuse. We also wonder about the wounds and unmet needs for love that came before the abuse and violence and led to the trauma and drama that terrorized a nation. Surely, Nichols' journey and the power of revealing it courageously in *Genesis* are not in vain. Surely, her journey is part of a larger plan to help those in need of similar assistance find their ways to healing, transformation, and renewal. For those who want and need it, this can be a new quest, a new beginning, a new genesis.

Four Love Quests by Darya Funches

What is the wound that has never fully healed?
What is the great lie and the truth the lie concealed?
What is the urgent dream that must be made real?
What is the part of you yearning most to be revealed?

Unleash Pure Love stored beneath the heart's great seal.
Circulate Pure Love within. Use all of your zeal.

Darya Funches, Ed.D. Author
I Send My Blankets Over You—Lessons of Love
November 27, 2007
"Four Love Quests" is a poem from the book,
I Send My Blankets Over You.

Genesis: The DC Sniper Story Untold

Foreword by Apostle Renee Taylor
Founder, Sister Nations

Pain, they say is the common denominator among all peoples. Each one of us can attest to the fact that we have experienced pain in our lives. Whether it is emotional, physical, or mental, pain is something that we have come to expect will happen over the course of our lifetime. We view it almost as we view accidents, it happens. We don't look forward to it, but we understand that into each life, some "rain" must fall. However, what happens when the pain occurs cannot be understood, when it does not fall into the category of the acceptable and understandable pain: i.e., a divorce, rejection, the loss of a loved one, or an unexplained illness. What happens when the pain occurs as the result of a deliberate and senseless act? When the pain is something that the mind cannot comprehend?

In *Genesis: The Untold Story of the D.C. Sniper*, Isa Farrington-Nichols reveals a life that is forever changed by this type of pain. When Isa asked me to review and then write the forward to *Genesis: The Untold Story of the D.C. Sniper,* I was deeply honored. I have had the pleasure of knowing Isa for many years; she has been and continues to be an important part of our family. I remember the first day that I met her, I was immediately, and acutely aware that she was the type of person that books are written about. She is not easily forgotten; primarily because she has a great ability to believe in people so much so that they believe in themselves. There were a number of times when Isa's "love in action," reminded me of who I am. She is doing the same with this book. *Genesis* is a labor of love to those who the world has forgotten due to the nature of their "unacceptable" pain. We as a society tend to shun those whose experience with pain doesn't make sense to us. We don't understand why a woman would remain or return to an abusive relationship, we don't know what to say to those who have experienced violent act towards themselves or the ones that they love.

Unfortunately, many are victimized again through our systems and its lack of understanding. As a result, they seek to hide and society settles into the safety of its understandable pain, continuing the cycle. With great courage and compassion, Isa has become the voice for the many victims who desire the cycle to be broken. She tells her extraordinary story in such a way that the most ordinary of us can understand that human dignity and grace can be restored, even after a time of unexplainable, unacceptable pain. Together, we can take the journey to victory!

Genesis: The DC Sniper Story Untold

Foreword By Maxine Buie Mimms, PhD

The title *Genesis* comes from the **Greek Γένεσις**, meaning "birth", "creation", "cause", "beginning", "source" or "origin." Isa Nichols in writing the book *Genesis: The Untold Story of the DC Sniper* describes a modern day Greek tragedy. This book simply reads like a play in ancient times, where unthinkable brutality was done to human beings on a daily basis for pleasure. The story unfolds long before these tragic victims became mental misfits. John Muhammad is a misfit, Lee Malvo is a misfit, and the governmental systems that are established to provide protection from them are governmental misfits. In this society, if we continue to provide an environment where domestic violence is incurred through our music, through our marriage vows, immature relationships, and lustful desires mistaken for love, we will continue to see an escalation of this brutish behavior.

Our most sacred institutions; church, home, and school are no longer the sanctuary for human discourse. Ms. Isa Nichols has provided us with a book that can start a necessary and a much needed conversation. The book provides us with an opportunity for self discovery so that each reader can disarm self. Violence is self hatred. Peace is self love. Ms. Isa Nichols has placed herself in the forefront of truth telling by writing this book.

Each page should obligate the reader to do something about domestic violence in your church, in your neighborhood, and in your home. One person can make a difference, as this is exactly what Ms Nichols has attempted to do in this book.

Maxine Buie Mimms, PhD
Founder, Evergreen State College — Tacoma Campus
Founder, Maxine Mimms Academies

Part One: In The Beginning
Introduction:

In order to tell this story, I have to tell a story of abuse, rage, betrayal, secrets, depression, mental challenges, family, friendship, and a story of the long road to healing. I continued to get phone calls from supportive friends. I began to return some of the calls. I began to start checking e-mails. One of those e-mails was from my good friend and former client Mildred Williams Muhammad. In 1994, the then Mildred Williams came into my tax office, which was located in the Hilltop of Tacoma, Washington.

Mildred Williams was average in height with a dark complexion, a beautiful bright smile, and her hair wrapped with a beautiful scarf. I could tell that she was Muslim, as her dress was significant to women of the Muslim faith. Muslim women wore attire that covered the hair down to the feet. I had a bookkeeping, tax preparation, and business-consulting firm. My office was on the main corridor of Martin Luther King Jr. Way in Tacoma. There were two traffic lights at both sides of MLK Way, and my office was between 12th and 13th streets. Mildred was driving down MLK Way toward 13th Street, when she noticed my accounting office. As she sat and waited for the light to turn green, she was able to read the services offered by my company, Nichols-Wright and Associates, on the window we had professionally designed to advertise our services in detail.

Mildred sat and waited for the light to change, then decided to take her car around the block, find a parking place, and come into the office. Mildred Williams was the owner of a small auto repair business. Her husband John Williams was the mechanic. She came into the office looking for information regarding our services and noticed I was what she called a "sistah," a term of endearment often used to refer to close female friends in the African-American community. Parking was not good at certain hours of the day. She had driven around the block to park her car, in front of my office. I looked out and saw a nice, clean, white Nissan 300ZX sports car. Out of the car came this very charming looking African-American female heading toward my doorway. I was not expecting any clients that day. I was just doing some data entry and writing letters. When she entered the office, she said, "Hello." I said, "Hello, how can I help you?" She extended her hand, which I shook, and she said, "You're an African-American." I said, "Last time I checked." We laughed and she introduced herself and I offered her a seat.

Mildred began to share with me that she and her husband John Williams lived in Tacoma and had started a car and truck repair business. They started the business from home and had recently moved the business to the Tacoma Small Business Incubator. She also said that their business was growing and she really needed some help with their bookkeeping and accounting. When she saw the advertising on the window, she felt it was a divine moment because she had been praying to Allah to provide resources for her for the things she needed for their business.

Mildred was extremely polite. I asked her if she had the proper business licensing for their business. She responded with a "yes, ma'am." She was so charismatic and respectful. I remember saying: "If you yes, ma'am me one more time, I was going to put you out of my office." We laughed and before she knew it, she had said yes, ma'am again. I knew then this was a very nice lady, and of course, I was willing to provide her with a comprehensive business development service package to insure the solid foundation needed for their business to grow. Growing startup businesses was my passion. It is promising when a client knows enough to seek professional services in order for their business to be profitable. She shared with me that her husband John Allen Williams served in the Army as a mechanic and was the mechanic for their mobile car repair business. She indicated that they wanted to start a business they could operate and leave as a legacy for their children.

I thought that her vision was very respectable, and definitely doable. They had a unique business idea and concept of repairing cars – a mobile car repair service – they came to you rather than you going to them. I felt that this concept was unique and it sounded very interesting to me. I knew that this concept was a niche and, with the right type of accounting and business planning, they could be extremely profitable.

I gave Mildred Williams a business card and brochure because she was anxious to go home and let her husband know that she had found an African-American accountant and business consultant. We set an appointment and I gave her a checklist of bookkeeping data and information that she should provide in order for me to begin bookkeeping for her. I let her know to call me if she had any questions or problems. I suggested that I meet her husband, as it was my job to train them on how to use their financial statements for their business. I told her that I took a holistic approach to my bookkeeping and accounting practice; I supplied administrative and management services linked with bookkeeping, tax, and accounting services.

When Mildred came back for the appointment, we signed a contract and went over the services that I was going to provide. The services included monthly bookkeeping, accounting, business and personal tax preparation, business consultation.. Then she paid me a retainer to start our contract. She provided all of the information that I had on the checklist. It was well organized and in chronological order, which led me to believe and supported my view that she was a very organized and detailed person. Her business communication skills were good. She articulated herself very well.

I began to enter the data and gave her a time frame in which I would have the information and reports for her to organize. I requested that her husband, John Williams, be in attendance, as I explained it was very important for them to use the financial statements as an inspection tool for their business, and that it was my job to train them how to use their financial statements. Then, we ended the appointment. Mildred was very ecstatic and gave me that beautiful smile. This time we embraced each other with a hug.

Her excitement and cheerfulness were contagious. It was always such a pleasure to have her come in and be so receptive to what I was saying as her accountant and consultant.

Meeting John Williams Muhammad:

Finally, the appointment came and in walked Mildred Williams with her husband, John Allan Williams. John Williams was very clean cut, tall, and very respectful. He introduced himself. Mildred and I embraced, and I asked them to sit down. John was very friendly and excited at the fact that Mildred had found an African-American accounting service to work with them. He let me know that his wife had told him about my services and that he was excited to be doing business with another black business. He avidly believed in supporting black businesses in the community, and said that if more black people supported and patronized black businesses, we would be some of the wealthiest citizens in America. I told him I agreed wholeheartedly.

I got the reports and a copy of the financial statements ready for the Williams. I began to show them the income that was generated, less the cost of the materials purchased and expenses, and what their net profit was. Their net profit was small, yet they were still operating with positive cash flow. I began to explain that the balance sheet was an actual picture of the company. John replied, "a picture of what?" and my comment was, "a picture of the assets, whether cash or inventory and loans; also the liabilities of the company, what the company owed to creditors; also any liability for accounts payable, and then the capital paid in money you had put into the business yourselves."

Mildred and John were very excited. Mildred explained that for the first time they were actually able to see the outcome of their effort. The numbers supported the hard work they put into the business. I also explained that we would analyze the next three months of reports to determine a pattern of spending and sales volume. The goal would be to find out how much they were spending for automobile parts and negotiate with their supplier to get a better price for parts according to volume, thus reducing their expense and increasing their profit. This was the first strategy laid out for Express Car/Truck Mechanic.

Express Car/Truck Mechanic was a sole proprietorship when they first contracted with me. Every month, Mildred Williams would call to make an appointment when she had gathered the receipting for the month. Every time she had gathered the receipts and organized them, she was very meticulous and detailed. She began to put the receipts in the order that I had them on the financial statements. I was impressed that she paid such attention to detail. Mildred served as the office administrator and dispatcher. She networked to bring in business. She handled all the day-to-day functions of the business. John was the mechanic, and would go to the appointments that Mildred had set up for him to do minor repairs on cars and trucks. Once a month, I would meet with John and Mildred to go over the financial statements and talk about ways to increase profits and reduce overhead.

From 1994 to 1998, I provided services and consulted John and Mildred in accounting and administration. We started developing a business plan, which included a marketing plan for contract work. The contract work was vital, as it would allow the business not to be solely dependent on just one avenue or method of generating revenue. In the marketing plan; we identified how they could carry out contract work for fleet vehicles such as rental cars, trucking businesses, any type of business that required the use of fleet automobiles. We devised a preventative maintenance package, which included services such as oil changes, lube, and tune-ups at a fixed price for fleet repairs.

This eventually became a very lucrative and steady source of income for the business. It increased the profit of Express Car/Truck Mechanic. Mildred was now getting the business more polished and mainstreamed in its attire and look. She ordered uniforms and designed stationary with a logo. She designed new branding for Express Car/Truck Mechanic. She had matching letterhead and business cards made up and put their logo on the uniforms. She designed their invoices and estimate sheets with the company's logo and branding. Within a few years, Express Car/Truck Mechanic became a household name. The service was so professional that Mildred gave evaluation cards to clients to make comments and rate the service provided. She realized that customer service and care was the vital piece needed for success in their business. I would always remind them that profit was not made by the sale of the service, but by the return of that client for service. We wanted the clients to come back for more services and to make referrals.

In four years, Express Car/Truck Mechanic went from a sole proprietorship to a corporation. They hired an assistant to help John in the field repairing cars. They hired an office receptionist. They hired an independent marketing consultant to implement the marketing and sales ideas found in the business plan. The consultant's primary role was to go on sales calls and get contracts from car and truck companies.

The Muhammad Family

John and Mildred had three young children, two girls and one son. Little John, Salena, and baby Taalibah. Taalibah was 15 months old when I first met the whole family. Mildred and I grew closer and our families became close as well. My oldest daughter, Tasherra, was a fill-in babysitter for Mildred's three children while Mildred and John worked the business.

I celebrate my birthday in April, and since it was also the end of tax season, I would entertain my clients as a thank you for their accounting and tax business. It was a way to say thank you for their support, because I really appreciated their business. I went all out for my birthday celebration, honoring my clients and networking for new ones. John and Mildred attended. John helped with the fish fry cookout. John and Mildred were Nation of Islam and did not eat red meat or pork. We had a good time.

Our relationship had grown to be so pleasurable that my family was invited to the Williams' family celebrations. I had the privilege of meeting Mildred's mother, Mrs. Olivia Green. Mrs. Olivia was in her late sixties and she was the primary care giver for the Williams children while John and Mildred worked 10 to 12-hour days. Mrs. Olivia loved her grandchildren. She came for the birth of Taalibah and remained with her daughter and son-in-law in their home. She was on Social Security and she had some medical illnesses. One of her illnesses was diabetes. She had also had a stroke. She was a stroke survivor.

Mrs. Olivia was a very strong and opinionated Christian woman. She was not Muslim, and did not waste any time letting you know that she was saved, sanctified, and filled with the Holy Ghost. When she found out I was a Christian, she would share with me often of the goodness of Jesus Christ to her. She loved her daughter very much. She loved John. But mostly, she really loved being around her grandchildren, especially Taalibah.

It was Mildred's decision not to allow her mother to be put in a nursing home, but to come and share in her life. It was not always easy, as Mildred was raised Christian and had recently converted to the Nation of Islam. This was quite a change from the Christian child Mrs. Olivia raised. Mrs. Olivia knew very little about the Muslim religion. Mrs. Olivia continued with her faith, praying in the name of Jesus. Mildred respected her mother and made sure that she got to church, prayer meetings, and anywhere else Mrs. Olivia needed to go.

I too, had my parent staying with me. My father, James Farrington, was a stroke victim, a stroke survivor. In 1993, I moved my father to Tacoma with me, to live with Joseph, my daughters, and me. My father's stoke came one week before his 60th birthday. He was retired after 20 years of truck driving. In his spare time, my father delivered lunches to senior citizens at noon. One day, he had got out of his truck and his leg began to drag, then he fell over. Fortunately, someone had seen him fall, and noticed that he was having a stroke. The paramedics were called and took him to the hospital. The stroke changed my father's entire life. The quality of his life, as he knew it, was now dependent on help from others. Eventually, my father moved to Washington and became a member of my immediate family. I had always told him I would be there for him whenever he needed me, that I would not abandon him. I told him always to remember that I would care for him. And I meant that.

Having to care for elderly parents was just another area in Mildred's and my life that we had some commonality. Both of our parents were demanding and in need. They both had critical medical conditions. And we were both youngest siblings taking care of our elderly parents.

Express Car/Truck Mechanic also handled the repairs of our personal vehicles. John repaired my mother in-law's vehicles, my vehicle, my husband's vehicle, and most of our friends, because we had referred them to our friends and acquaintances. We had shared their service and their concept with just about everyone we knew that needed car repair service. When John would come by the house to do a repair or to do a tune-up, he would talk with my father. My father loved to talk, and the fact that John knew a lot about cars and trucks was intriguing to my father. As a retired truck driver of 20 years, my father and John would talk for at least an hour. John would totally entertain my father with conversation. My father enjoyed every time John would come by. My father would roll his wheelchair up to John and engage him in conversations about trucks. He was so respectful, calling my father "sir," and would always respond with a "yes, sir" and "no, sir." My father admired John as a hard working businessman with a beautiful family, and would tell John this as if he was his son.

My father enjoyed Mildred when she would come to our home. My father could never get the names of Mildred and John's daughters correct. He finally gave up, and just asked how the "Shebas" were, which would mean Salena and Taalibah. Mildred and I would just laugh, and she would respond that they were just fine. When the children were around, they were just as respectful with "no, sir" and "no, ma'am" and "yes, sir" and "yes, ma'am." They were so intelligent and very articulate. They were beginning readers. They were readers before they went to school.

John Jr. was treated as John's second in command. His daughters were treated as African queens, daddy's African Queens. He would oftentimes refer to them as "his queens." Mildred was very passionate about her family, and she loved her husband very much. She wanted the business to be successful and her husband to be a proud, successful, black man in the eyes of the community, in the eyes of his family, and in the eyes of their Mosque. They were avid Nation of Islam followers. They were devout and dedicated to the Nation of Islam. They worshipped at the Mosque on Sundays and John and Mildred were both very involved with Nation of Islam affairs. Mildred held a district leadership position at the Mosque. They both served in their Mosque with much dedication and pride.

I remember the phenomenal event of the Million Man March that Minister Louis Farrakhan called in Washington D.C. John Williams attended the Million Man March. Mildred was so proud, and so was I, because the Million Man March allowed black men in America to atone to their families, their mothers, their sisters, and their community. However, it was not just a Muslim event; it was a call for every black man in America to be at the nation's capitol. Mildred invited me over; I made a decision to not work in the office and watch this historical event in the comfort of her home. I gladly accepted her invitation and watched the unfolding of a very historic moment in our African-American culture and the world.

We shared a sense of solidarity, although I was Christian and believed in the Trinity, and in Jesus Christ as the Messiah and Savior. We sat there, from the early hours of the morning into the late part of the evening. I remember looking in the crowd on television, looking to see if we saw John. We knew that this was a time in history when people of all religious beliefs were coming together. We watched the most powerful display of black men –

something that just had not been seen before. There was no criminal activity. It was true empowerment.

They did a demonstration of how powerful our economic power in this country was by asking every black man to hold up a dollar. They asked every person to pass the dollar to the man behind them. We watched on television as over one million men passed at least a million dollars through everyone's hands. Mildred and I sat there, holding each other's hands, looking at this exercise of economic power going through our black men's hands. We were speechless.

When John returned from the Million Man March, I wanted to hear everything John had to say regarding the historical occasion. I remember wishing that my husband, Joseph, could have attended. He was away in Korea, but he had watched the Million Man March broadcast. I often wondered if Joseph was here in America, would he have made the journey to Washington, D.C. to experience the march. Would it have made a difference in his life? Would he be willing to atone for his mistreatment of me? Would it have deposited something in him that could be of value? I would have paid anything to get him there!

From 1994 until 1998, my client Express Car/Truck Mechanic had grown. They were now doing annual sales in the six digits with just one mechanic and a couple of assistants. I filed their reports and taxes and made sure that they understood them. I made sure that John and Mildred understood the importance of paying sales tax and income taxes, so that the tax agencies would not have to be a problem. Many African-American businesses would make the mistake of co-mingling sales taxes with operations and when it was time to pay they did not have the money and I did not want Express Car/Truck Mechanic to fall into this same trap.

Over time something began happening in their business. The Williams began to have problems in their business. John began missing appointments. The financial statements began to reveal inconsistencies in parts purchased and cash received. One day, Mildred received a disturbing phone call from a female client. She was calling to ask to speak to the owner of the company. Most people thought that John was an employee because he had a uniform with his name, John, sewn on a patch. He looked as if he was just an average employee. Mildred made all calls and appointments, and so the public just assumed that John was an employee, and not the owner. When this particular call came in, Mildred explained that she was the owner, and the woman began to complain that John was stalking her, and soliciting her for sex. She wanted to file a complaint and was considering a lawsuit against Express Car/Truck Mechanic for the misconduct of their employee, John Williams.

Mildred called me to share the nature of the client's complaint. Clients were also saying that they had paid John in cash. However, Mildred never saw the cash, or the deposits of the cash into the business account. When Mildred confronted John about the phone call, he denied it, and said that the woman was trying to pay him with sexual favors for fixing her car. He was angry that she called and made up a lie against him. John was angry, and resented the speculation from this complaint.

By this time, Mildred had contracted with a marketing professional that had extensive experience in sales and marketing. He had worked for Fortune 500 companies, received awards, and was recognized for his sales volume and expertise. He was also a good friend of John and Mildred. Mildred had asked if he would follow-up on the woman's complaint. He was very professional in his attire. He was a Christian man who was very ethical and very well spoken. He, of course, was very concerned and wanted to do whatever he could do to assist Mildred in this complaint. He called the client and arranged to meet with her to further investigate her complaint. This strategy was very instrumental in assisting Mildred in saving the Express Car/Truck Mechanic's image. But, nonetheless, things continued to get worse.

John continued to miss appointments. He was showing signs of resentment and speculation around the business' rapid growth. Mildred had shared with me that John was not in places where he needed to be, and she did not know of his whereabouts at certain times. There were times when John didn't come home until the next day. Things just weren't adding up. Of course, with John being the only mechanic, this affected the company's ability to generate revenue. In addition, it affected their ability to support their household. Bills began to pile up, both at home and at the business. It got to the point where Mildred could no longer afford to pay for my services.

In four years, this was the first time that she was not able to pay for my services. So I did not want to abandon her in this time. It was my feeling that this was just going to be a short phase, and they would get back on track with things. I provided Mildred with instructions on how to continue the record keeping. She pretty much had done the work, and had a system in place that she could manage the record keeping on her own and then just come to me to get the yearly reports and file their taxes annually, or quarterly. Without the main burden of paying for record keeping, she was able to keep me on an as-needed basis. I continued to support Mildred with consulting on some of the business problems, which continued to multiply.

In 2000-2001, I did not hear very much from Mildred or her family. I, too, at this time was going through some transition with my life. I had been separated from my husband and in 1999, he returned from a tour duty in Korea. We decided to reconcile and put our family back together. It was in 2000 that I began to have to re-focus my energy into the reconciliation of my marriage. I had to make a lot of adjustments in my business and my practice. I wanted more than anything for my marriage to work. For the first time, I put my marriage before everything, making it a priority. I felt I needed to show my husband that he was a priority. I wanted him to know that I loved and respected him.

My business changed: I ended a profitable four-year business partnership with my partner Tony Wright, and I was no longer Nichols-Wright and Associates, but Nichols and Associates. I no longer had an office; instead, I worked from home to be available to my family.

The American Dream

Nichols and Associates is the name of my business. I was the only African-American independent public accountant in the Tacoma, Pierce County area. There were other accountants, but most worked on jobs. I was expanding again. I was interested in growing my business and diversifying into other areas. I wanted to get into residential mortgage lending. Tax season was ending and the time was good for me to look into that industry. Tax planning and home ownership were becoming more appealing to me.

Joseph Nichols and I were separated again and living in two separate homes. Although we were separated in location, we continued to care for one another. We would sleep together. That part of the marriage was not one of our issues. This went on for years. For some reason it did not bother me. Whenever I needed Joseph, he would be there. Often times, he would be there when I hadn't called. We were really good friends. We loved each other and we knew that. We loved our children even more. Neither one of us mentioned divorce. I conducted my life as the wife of Joseph Nichols, despite our married, but separate, lifestyle.

In 1997, I found a beautiful new home that was for sale by the owner-builder. I qualified to buy the home, but in order to get a better interest rate and loan to value ratio, I needed to show more income. I asked Joseph if he would sign on the documents, so that I could include his income. I had him meet me at the house so that he could see it. I convinced him that the girls and I needed a home. We could both purchase homes and give them each a home. Joseph loved our daughters. He would do anything for them. The loan program that I was qualifying for was a conventional loan program.

Joseph could use his VA benefits to get him a home later on. Joseph did not think that I could afford the house; I had informed him that I had started a contract that was paying me $5,000 per month and that I would use his financial support for the girls. The strategy made sense to him and he agreed to sign on the documents. The loan closed escrow in October 1997 and my daughters, my father, and I moved into our new home. Things were going according to plan. I wished I had my husband there to share it. I wanted to be like other married couples buying their first home.

In 1998, Joseph went to Korea for a one-year Army tour of duty. It was his third assignment in Korea. While there, we started talking about reuniting our family. He said he wanted to come back home. Although I was nervous, I did want him back. I still loved him. I believed that God could do anything and that included healing broken marriages. I believed I could do anything through Christ strengthening me. When his tour of duty was over, we decided that he would come home to our girls and me. In October 1999, Joseph and I reunited from a four-year marital separation. We were now in, or approaching, our 40s in age. I believed that Joseph's desire to party all the time had run its course. It had run its course for quite a while. I could forgive the infidelities. I had done so many times in the past. Forgiveness is a gift. I was gifted when it came to forgiveness.

The 2000 millennium New Year was approaching. I looked forward to New Years. I liked the fact that they were brand new. I did not enter into a new year without setting some goals and expectations. I would pray to God for his will to be manifest in my life. I would pray for myself, that God continue to strengthen me. I had not spent a New Years with Joseph in a few years. Whatever he wanted to do was going to be all right with me. I prepared for whatever he wanted to do. In the past, I would be at the watch meeting service at church. I loved being there.

However, in 2000, I was going to do whatever my husband wanted to do. Since he had just come back from Korea, he wanted to go to a small house gathering with his family and friends. We often partied a lot with my in-laws. They loved to party and there was no excuse needed to throw one. I dressed up in some terrific looking clothes. Earlier, I went and did the salon thing, so my hair was stylish and on point. My nails were manicured and my feet were pedicured. I bought a little negligee for when we got home. I really wanted this New Years to be special.

The party was going on. I wanted to be at church attending the watch service. Watch service was a tradition in my family. My mother and father would take us to church at 9:00 pm on New Years Eve. We would pray, praise, and worship in the New Year. After the service, they would serve breakfast. We would spend the first hours of the New Year in fellowship. My heart was really there. I had a lot to thank God for. Partying on a New Year's Eve just did not interest me anymore. The word of God requires a wife to be of the world to attend to the needs of her husband. I would have rather been home with Joseph in my negligee with a bottle of Asti Spumante. When the midnight hour came, I made my way to where Joseph was. I stared at him as he was hollering and counting down. I hoped and really believed that the New Year was going to be a good year. We had overcome so much. When midnight hit, I turned with my eyes closed and waited to kiss him. When I opened my eyes, he had left me standing there. Was that an indication of what my 2000 was going be like? Oh my God!

In 2000, I lost my $5,000 per month paying contract, my father took very ill, and had to move into a nursing home, which took his income with him. The financial woes were back. Joseph was back to his disappearing acts. We had managed to get our eldest daughter away to attend college at St. Augustine's College in Raleigh, North Carolina. I had so much on my emotional plate that my doctor warned me I would be dead in my grave and my father would still be here. That got my attention. Since I had lost my contract and the income that came from my father was going to the nursing home, I needed to re-think some stuff. We were in our second bankruptcy, so the house and property tax payment were paid through it. Joseph was depressed and angry most of the time. It was the typical glass empty versus glass full scenario. I thought the Chapter 13 was a resource that saved our home. I was grateful to God that we had something valuable to save through a bankruptcy. Joseph was disgusted and embarrassed about the Chapter 13 Bankruptcy. He was appalled that it was our second time, and to Joseph, it was my entire fault.

In October 2001, I took a job. I wanted to see if it would make a difference in Joseph's behavior. Would it bring him home at night? Would I get his respect? Nope! I started to work for All Fund Mortgage in Spanaway, Washington as a contract loan processor to a loan officer.

Pamela Martinez was the branch manager. Pamela had a white girl sounding voice, a Hispanic last name, but she was a dark skinned, beautiful African-American female in Spanaway. It was a family run business. Naturally, this impressed me. I interviewed with Pamela and was hired. I went into training as a processor and loan officer. I didn't let anyone know of my experience in accounting, or that I had a tax practice. It was all about learning the residential mortgage industry. I was excited to be on their team. Pamela knew her business. She had business savvy and worked long hours. This quality we both had. I listened to every word she said. I wanted to know what she knew about the business.

I believe in surrounding myself with positive people. I mirrored her, even to the point that I started wearing these cute ponytails in my hair. They were neat and convenient. I was always a low maintenance hair kind of person anyway. Pamela's office was predominately white. Her mother Ms. Frankie and her sister were the only African-American women I saw most of the time. Again, I was impressed by a sister girl running her business with predominately white staff. Oh, I was having a blast.

On the home front, things were stable. My niece Keenya had just recently moved in the home with us with her five-month old baby girl. My home was a refuge to many. I shared with my husband that I wanted to expand my business to include mortgages. His reactions were usual. He was not interested. Here he was at Fort Lewis with hundreds of soldiers and did very little to send business my way. Imagine the VA loan lending potential. I could never get Joseph to understand that my business was worthwhile. That it could be better if I had his support. If I wasn't bringing home a bi-weekly paycheck, then it did not carry any value to him. He often compared me to female soldiers. He respected them because they went to work every day. He respected any female that went to work on an 8 to 5 every day. He just did not value entrepreneurialism. He made me aware of it every chance he could.

Joseph blamed me for our financial problems. It was my fault that we did not have any savings. It was my fault that we had filed two bankruptcies. It was my fault that he didn't have the rank he wanted. I was not the woman he wanted to come home to, so he didn't come home. There were times when I had to look in the closet to make sure he had not moved out. I was not the type of woman that would go on a stake out to find out where my husband was or whom he was with. I didn't have that kind of time. I had my daughters and I was very much involved in their lives. I had the comfort of my home and my children.

Whenever I would ask Joseph anything about his whereabouts, he would tell me it was none of my business. If I asked him for money, he would say when I started making some money, then I could ask him for some. He could be verbally abusive and cold hearted. When he really wanted to insult me, he would call me a dumb ass. He knew I had two bachelors degrees, so dumb ass was when he really wanted to get me angry, which gave him a reason to leave the house. Joseph was gone four out of seven days of the week at nightclubs or hanging out with "the fellas." To this day, I don't know what man would want to hang out with the guys until 4 and 5 a.m. in the morning. This is where he would say he had been. I know one thing, and that is infidelity is expensive. I knew that he was out with other women. That was why he never had any savings.

I was not the type to let anyone know that I was struggling to keep the marriage together. When he came home, he was wreaking with alcohol. It was just through prayer and the grace of God that he made it home. I would always be awake. I never could sleep when he wasn't home. Believe it or not, I worried about him being out there in the street. I worried if he was laying somewhere needing medical attention. Excessive drinking and driving is so dangerous.

An Abduction

One afternoon, I stopped by to see my friend Mildred out of the clear blue. She just popped into my heart. I happened to be in the neighborhood when I decided to just stop in. I pulled into the driveway, and I saw the front door open. I walked up and knocked on the door. I saw a silhouette of her and a man standing in the house. I knocked on the door, Mildred answered the door, and she asked me to come in. She was quite surprised, as I had not seen her in almost a year. Mildred was in her house with her brother. Her brother stopped by from time to time, as he was a truck driver. Whenever he was in town, he would make it a point to stop in and check on his sister, his mother, and the family.

One of the things I noticed that was strange was that the children were not running around to greet me. It was quiet. It was very quiet. So I asked Mildred where the children were. Then there was this stare. When I asked her where the children were again, she looked very worried. She stated that John had taken them and that he was supposed to have brought them home. My immediate response was when are they coming back. I was going to sit down as I had some time to kill, but I realized that she was really worried. So I asked her what she meant by "supposed to bring them home."

It was at this time that I found out that Mildred and John had separated in early 2000 and that he was no longer living in their home. I found out that John would get his children for weekend visitations that were arranged by him and Mildred during the separation.

Mildred explained to me that it was Mrs. Olivia's birthday, and that John had picked the children up from school, and that the last thing that she told

John was to bring the children back so they could have cake and ice cream for their grandmother's birthday. He agreed. Well, it was now many hours later and she had not heard anything from them. So, as I sat down with her, she began to share with me information about the threats. She began to share with me why she was concerned.

Mildred looked so fearful I immediately got the impression that something was terribly wrong. Her brother had to leave and told his sister he would give her call, and Mildred and I sat in the living room. I was just totally in shock, and I didn't want to leave Mildred. I asked how Mrs. Olivia was doing, and she said that she was okay, but she, too, was worried about the children.

As we sat there, to see if we were going to hear anything, waiting and looking at the telephone to see if it would ring, wondering and hoping that John would call to say that he was on his way, Mildred began to explain to me the events of their separation. She began to share with me her fear at the time, that in February 2000, John had tried to enter their home to see their son, because he was sick. And she had told him that he could not see him because he was asleep. She told me that John pushed his way into the house and pushed her out of the way. She then ran back and called 911 for the police to come. When they arrived, the police officers said there was nothing they could do without a restraining order. Mildred began to explain to me so many crazy things, so many peculiar things that John was doing. She mentioned that before that incident, John came to the house around 7 a.m. to inform her that he had tapped the phone lines. He said that the information he had would destroy her. He started threatening her and from then on, she began to feel extremely unsafe. Then the day after the police had come, John came over and informed her that he would not let her raise their children. This is exactly the day after she called 911 to file a complaint.

Based on our conversation, I now understood why Mildred was so intense and fearful. I understood why she felt that something was terribly wrong.

The only thing I could think of was to have her notify the police if she really felt that John had done something with the children. I asked her if there was a restraining order, and she informed me that she had filed a restraining order with the court. I told her that was one of the best things she could have done because, John's irrational behavior needed to be on record. John repeatedly violated the restraining order.

Mildred went in again the next month, which was sometime in March, and filed another restraining order because John was still threatening and calling her, threatening to destroy her life. She informed the court that she had to change her telephone number three times within five days, and that she had spoke with a representative at U.S. West Communications, the telephone company, and that person said that, according to their records, John called that day trying to find out her phone number. The telephone company sympathized with Mildred and had a special code on her phone records. Because of that code, John wasn't able to get the number.

Mildred again told the court that she was afraid of John. She said that John was a demolition expert in the military, and that he was behaving very irrationally. Whenever he talked to her, he said that he was going to destroy her life, and then he would hang up the phone. Now here we were sitting in her living room, thinking the worst of the worst. I began to try to strategize and give Mildred resources as to what she could do as we waited to see if the telephone would ring, and we waited to see if John was going to bring the children back. It was now well after 8 p.m. and there was still no word from John or the children. John never brought the children home.

As I went home to my family, there was such a nervous and empty feeling in my stomach regarding the possibility that John had taken their children, Mildred's children. After hearing of the dissolution of their marriage, and hearing the hopeless, sordid details of their separation, and listening to the harassment and the constant threats, I was greatly concerned as well. I began to pray that those children would be safe, and that there would be an explanation and that somehow those children would be home. I felt that John would just be playing a mean game just to scare Mildred.

I got a call from Mildred the next morning. She had contacted the police. John had called later on that evening and said that he and the children had been at K-Mart shopping. He was getting them something to eat, and would be bringing them home shortly. John never returned with the children. Two, three days later, John still failed to show up, nor call about his whereabouts or the children. Mildred began to get together more information. She found out the children's savings accounts were closed, and that John had taken the money out of each child's account.

Each child had about $300. She also found out that John had contacted the landlord and told him that he was no longer living there, and was no longer responsible for the payments on the house. She filed a complaint with the police that her children were missing, but there was nothing else we could do. All the information we found out she gave to the police authorities. She provided the police with pictures of the children, what they looked like. She contacted the school that the children attended to find out what time the children were picked up. The school confirmed that their father picked them up.

Mildred later discovered a real blow, the final blow. The police could not do very much because John was the father, and that the children were in his custody, were in his care, and that, because there was no custody agreement, that he had a right to be with the children, and therefore had not violated any laws. Of course, this did not set well and I just could not allow her to just sit there and accept that. I stressed the importance of her to get an attorney so that she could find out exactly what her rights were.

I could not understand how he could have rights to the children at the expense of her rights. Why couldn't the authorities act – my question was, and always will be – why couldn't the authorities act on the fact that these children were missing, bring them in and let the courts decide, or put them in foster care until the courts could decide the custodial plan for these children? Why couldn't the authorities take Mildred's statement that these children were taken, and that she had not heard from them? Why was that not enough to start an investigation. Why couldn't they bring them in to protective custody and let John and Mildred go before the judge to get their parenting issues handled. No one should have rights at the expense of the other. If one parent has said something contrary, then law enforcement must act expeditiously to get the missing children until a family judge can decide. Acting at the onset of a report could save lives.

Mildred's tornado, or twister, of horror only continued. She eventually got a notice of eviction from the landlord. I asked her how far behind she was in the payments. I happened to have some money in my savings. I contacted the landlord and told him that I could catch the payment up. But he would not accept it. He said that he wanted to sell the property, and so therefore, he denied our request to let Mildred live in the house. Mildred and I both pleaded with the landlord, telling him that John had taken the children, and telling him how important it would be that she remains there because that was the last known address the children knew. They children knew their entire address, including zip code, and they knew the telephone number.

We tried to convince him that her children had been abducted and by her not being in the home would hinder the possibility of the children finding her. To no avail, he proceeded with his request for her to vacate his property. I told Mildred to stay in the house as long as she could while looking for someplace else. The eviction process was not something that would occur in a couple of days, but in about 3 or 4 weeks the eviction would be final in court.

Life Interrupted

It was now critical. Pain and mania was a reality for Mildred. I wanted to be optimistic. It was hard to believe that John had done this, especially done this to his children. As days would go by, Mildred would update me. Our conversations always began with "have you heard from John about the children?" I was hoping for some sign that this was not really abduction. I wanted to believe that it was some type of cruel joke. In addition to all this, Mrs. Olivia was feeling the effects of her grandchildren being missing. John had spoken with her when he phoned the house and made comments that he was going to destroy her daughter. She had to awaken everyday and see the fearful, morbid look on her baby girl's face. She was afraid that John would follow through on the many threats that he made about destroying Mildred. She had every right to be fearful. She lived in the home and witnessed most of John's violent, aggressive, and abusive treatment of her daughter.

Over time, financial resources were getting thin. Mildred had no income. John had taken all the money. Mrs. Olivia lived off her social security benefits, which wasn't a whole lot. She made sure that they had the necessities. I tried to do whatever I could do to support and sustain them. My financial resources were not that great. I would give Mildred $30 or $40 to help with her bills or for whatever she needed. Financial issues were big issues in my marriage. I just prayed that my husband would understand. When I told him what was going on with Mildred, he was supportive. He didn't appear to be irritated. It somehow took my mind off my own marital problems.

With the eviction approaching, something had to be done. Where were they going to go? How were the children going to contact home? It was the only home that the children knew how to get to. Mildred, Mrs. Olivia, and I prayed without ceasing. Mildred prayed to Allah. Mrs. Olivia and I prayed in Jesus' name for a miracle. I didn't know how Muslims felt about miracles. But, I knew that God was a miracle maker, and we needed one soon.

Mother's Day 2001

It was now early May 2001. I had a client named Patricia that was a mental health professional with her own practice. I was worried because one of the children's birthday was approaching so I contacted Patricia. Patricia told me to bring Mildred to the office.

Patricia sat with Mildred and I. Mildred shared with her how John had abducted her children from school. Patricia listened intently. Little did we know that Patricia's children had been taken away by their father. She shared her story of what she did to cope until she got them back. I remember her telling Mildred that she should continue to celebrate the children's birthday; that she should buy gifts and wrap them, so when they returned, they would see that she hadn't forgotten about them. I thought that was a wonderful idea.

Patricia focused on how Mildred was coping while going through this ordeal. She was confident that Mildred would be reunited with her children. In the meantime, Mildred had to ask herself each day the question of what and where she would be when they are found. Would she be ready to step in and take them? That was really thought provoking. I wanted to remember to ask that question to Mildred in the future.

Patricia was an angel with wings that day for me. I offered to pay Patricia for her services, but she provided the consultation pro-bono for Mildred. Patricia encouraged us to stay in contact. She wanted to see Mildred again. Mildred followed Patricia's advice. The next thing I knew, Mildred had developed a web site, where she had scanned the latest school pictures of her children on there. She had also gotten an 800 number and a pager, so anyone could contact her with information about her children. Now her children were on the World Wide Web as missing children. A good idea!

Mother's Day was approaching. I constantly reminded her that she had to take care of herself. I noticed she wasn't eating. She did not have an appetite. Mildred was anemic. Once at her office, she fainted and had to be taken to the hospital. The stress and humiliation had begun to take control. All I could think about was how difficult it was going to be for Mildred to wake up on Mother's Day without her children. She was going to be miserable. I felt something in my spirit that something major was going to happen.

The Saturday before Mother's Day I wanted to call Mildred, however I had much anxiety about what to say. How could I ask how was she doing? How would I be doing if one day my children were gone, vanished without a trace? All I could do was pray that that they were protected and brought back safely. I was restless the entire day and I did not get any sleep. I cared about Mildred. I cared about Mrs. Olivia.

Then it was Mother's Day and I was getting ready to go to church with my family when the telephoned rang. It was Mrs. Olivia Green, Mildred's mother. She said that she needed my help. She asked me to go the emergency room at St. Joseph's Hospital. Mildred was taken there by ambulance. I asked if she wanted me to come and pick her up to take her there. She firmly said "no, I need you to go." I will never forget the fear in her voice as she pleaded with me to go. I told her I would get over to the hospital right away.

I told my husband about the phone call. I told him I would meet him and my daughter at church. He knew something was wrong. He cautioned me to calm myself and drive carefully. I asked him to pray. He said that he would.

When I arrived at the emergency room, Mildred was on a gurney in a small room behind a curtain. I went inside the room behind the curtain. Our eyes met and then she began to cry. She started apologizing to me for not taking care of herself. She said that she really tried. As tears filled her big eyes, she took on the look of her youngest baby girl Taalibah. Mildred looked like a frightened little girl. I stroked her head gently. We both were crying. We cried tears of fear, defeat, and frustration. Once I was able to get my composure, I tried to console her. I had to let her know that she was taking the best care of herself that she could. I commended her and told her how proud I was of her. I told her that I loved her. I told her that I would be there for her and we were going to get through this.

Mildred told me that there was a knock at her front door. She answered the door to find the postman there to deliver a package to Mrs. Olivia. It was sent there from one of her sisters for Mother's Day. The postman gave her a clipboard for her to sign for the package. That was the last thing that she remembered. The next thing she knew she was in an ambulance heading for the hospital. The postman told the ambulance personnel that after signing for the package, she fell back on the floor hitting her head very hard. He then ran back to his jeep to get his cell phone and dialed 911. Mrs. Olivia came to the front and saw her daughter lying on the floor. The postman explained to her what had happened. The ambulance arrived and took her to the hospital.

The nurse came to check on Mildred and said that she was going to take some X-rays. They felt she might have had a concussion from the fall. She said that they had to run blood tests after the X-rays. I decided to stay until it was time for her to go.

Suddenly the curtains were whisked back and a woman entered. She was dressed in Muslim attire. She walked in front of me as if I was invisible. She didn't say excuse me or hello. I just stood there in curiosity. She bent over to Mildred and said, "Beloved, how are you?" I was standing there in awe when Mildred introduced me as her friend, and said that they worship at the same mosque. She finally said hello. She continued to talk to Mildred, to act as if I wasn't there; as if she was waiting for me to leave the room. I wasn't going anywhere! I had to see what this spirit was about.

Mildred began to explain to her what little she remembered, which was very little. I wasn't going to give up any information. Her countenance was all wrong. I just waited quietly, watching her every move. My spirit just made me stay put. She kept asking Mildred all these questions. Had she heard from John? Mildred told her that some one kept calling the house and hanging up. She felt it was John.

My thinking was confused. I remember Mildred sharing with me that she had gone to her sisters at the mosque for help and support during some of the most difficult times in her marriage. She felt that she and John needed counseling. I don't remember her saying that she received any. John and Mildred separated one day. John went to the elders at the mosque and told them that Mildred was not a good wife; that she was having an affair.

Apparently, they believed him because she was removed from a position that she had held in the organization. They had begun to align themselves with John and they believed his accusations of adultery. I didn't understand how the organization would take such a drastic position based on an accusation. Mildred later informed me that John had wire tapped the telephone line and tape-recorded a telephone conversation that she had with a male friend. John took the tape to the mosque and played it to them. Shortly thereafter, she was removed from her position. I didn't know much about the Nation of Islam other than my exposure with the Muhammads practicing in it. I knew of some other Muslims in the community. A few were business clients of mine. I did know one thing, and that was that this Islamic sister's rudeness came through and made me a bit skeptical.

The nurse came back to get Mildred and took her for X-rays and a CAT scan. I told Mildred that I would return later after I return from church. Her friend left. I walked down the hospital corridor with Mildred. I just had to make sure she was okay. I left the hospital and went to join my family. I called Mrs. Olivia on the telephone and told her that Mildred was stable. I assured her that Mildred was not in any immediate danger and that she was being well taken care of. I asked if she needed anything. Did she want me to come by the house? She said no. I told her that I was going back to the hospital later. Mrs. Olivia was traumatized with worry.

I finally arrived at church. I went in and sat next to my family. I was exhausted. I was emotionally overwhelmed. My church was having a Mother's Day program. I glanced at all the mothers in the church. It then hit me that there were mothers like Mildred that did not know where there children were. I looked at my beautiful daughter. I was so proud of both my girls. I then looked at my husband. I stared at him for a little while. Although we were in turmoil trying to make our marriage work, he had not resulted to anything that would severe our children away from me. I thank God for that. While he often could be emotionally abusive, he did not involve our girls. I seldom exposed any one of them to my emotional pain and suffering. I just didn't. I often prayed to God to restore our marriage. I prayed that he would touch our hearts and heal our hurts. I knew of no other way to endure difficult times, other than prayer. Prayer changes things. Prayer can get into places that no one else can. That is what I believe.

On the way home, I shared what I had experienced. By the time that I finished, we all felt sorrowful about the situation. We arrived home and began my Mother's Day celebration. My husband prepared dinner. My daughters had lavished me with gifts and their love. I enjoyed the rest of my Sunday.

As the evening arrived, I called the hospital to check on Mildred. They informed me that she had been admitted to the fifth floor. When I got to Mildred's room she had IVs running out her arm. She looked much better. She said that the doctor said she was extremely dehydrated and her blood pressure was low. Her blood count was anemic. Mildred had been given three pints of blood. She said that she had told her doctors about her turmoil. I was glad that she had confided in them.

I knew Mildred needed some serious help. She needed professional help and now she could possibly get some referrals. I was hoping that she could get access to the hospital's staff psychiatrist and social worker. I asked her if she wanted to seek counseling. She said she hadn't really considered it. This episode was definitely an eye opener. She would have to have some type of support when she left the hospital. She could no longer go on bearing the many burdens any more. I was convinced that this was not going to get any better.

Mildred was spiraling downward more and more. I was concerned about her mother. Mildred could not take care of herself, let alone take care of her ailing mother. The eviction was just ahead. I had to find away to approach the subject. Where were they going to go? Mildred was too sick to get a job. She needed to get some income. I asked Mildred if she had contacted her other sisters. One lived in Texas, and one lived in Maryland. I knew we had to get Mrs. Olivia to one of them. Mildred knew that Mrs. Olivia could be stubborn and would not want to move. Mildred called her sisters. She too realized that she needed to get her mother to live with one of them. She had a lot of things to consider and figure out. The hospital social worker came to speak with Mildred. I was glad.

Hysterical and Homeless

On Monday morning, I woke up with much anxiety. I had a full day of business clients to serve, a home to run, and a teenage daughter to care for. I got on my knees and started talking to God. I had to thank him first and foremost for allowing me to see another day. Gradually I felt better. The more I talked to God the lighter I felt, so I stayed there in His presence for a while longer. I didn't want to get up until I knew that God had restored me with strength and courage.

I called Mrs. Olivia to see how she was doing. She still did not want to go to the hospital to see Mildred; she said she was tired. Mildred had called her and she had spoken with her. Mrs. Olivia tried to assure me that she was going to be okay. I asked her if she had been taking her medication. Now was not the time for her to get sick. She told me she had. She thanked me for being such a good friend to her daughter. She thanked me for my prayers, and for being a woman of God. I too thanked her for being kind and loving to me. She asked me if I was going back up to the hospital, I said of course. She seemed relieved.

I arrived at the hospital to find Mildred sitting up in bed. She still was receiving IV fluids in her arm. She looked very well and rested. I sat down and we began to talk when the telephone ranged. She answered it; it was

John calling. All I could hear was her comments. She was asking calmly where the children were. Could she please speak to the children?

"John please let me speak to them. Why are you keeping the children from me? They need their mother. Please!" Mildred began to cry. She then started screaming hysterically, "No! No! No! John, No!"

Mildred was screaming so loud the nursing staff came running in. She was kicking and screaming. The IV came out of her arm. They looked at me for answers. I was standing there with my mouth open and tears in my eyes. I just looked back at them. I think I was in shock. They asked me again what happened. I said it was her husband on the phone. He has taken her children away and no one has helped her get them back. Mildred was screaming, "He is going to kill me!" "He is coming; he is coming to kill me!" "No, no, don't let him kill me!" She said he is going to kill my mother. Mildred was crying and so hysterical that they put in an order for a sedative.

The hospital staff took the threats seriously and immediately called the Tacoma Police Department. They also moved her to another room on another floor. They took her name off the patient directory. They posted hospital security outside her hospital door. All visitors had to sign in and show picture identification. The police arrived and took Mildred's statement on what happened. This was not the first complaint filed against John by Mildred. She had filed at least two restraining orders previously with the department for this same type of harassment and threats against her life. However, this time, the police were more inclined to her complaint. She told them everything he said. They sent a patrol car out to her house to check on Mrs. Olivia. Mrs. Olivia told them that John had called her and threatened to kill her daughter. Finally, they were going to issue a warrant for his arrest.

Mildred was in real turmoil. I stayed with her as the medication started to calm her. We began to talk again. I would never forget what had just happened that day. Never! There was something bothering me. How did

John know that Mildred was in St. Joseph's hospital? At the time the only people that knew she was in there was her mother, her friend from the mosque, and me. I asked Mildred whom else did she call. She said she called some of her sister's at the mosque. She said she wanted to see if she could get some protection for herself. The ministry had some type of security people called FOI within their organization. She said she had spoken to one of their husbands. It was apparent and clear to me that someone called John. They knew how to reach him. Mildred said that John even knew she had received three pints of blood.

I found it difficult to understand how she thought that the people that refused to provide her marital support and removed her from her position would lift a finger to help her and the children. Mildred went to many of them asking if they had seen John with the children. They told her no. It was obvious to me that these people knew John had taken the children from their mother. Someone had been in communication with him since he had abducted them. I was appalled at the fact that they would condone such behavior; that they would condone children being taken from their mother. These were people that Mildred and John worshiped and fellowshipped with. The fact that some of these people are the same people I provided business services to made me feel uncomfortable. What could Mildred have possibly done to make her friends turn their backs on her?

I felt someone in the ministry should have supported her. Someone should have given her the benefit of the doubt. Someone in their ministry should have tried to restore this family. Why was I the only one helping her anyway? I stayed at the hospital most of the day and rescheduled my appointments. I was already exhausted and my day hadn't really got under way.

The hospital social worker came in to talk to Mildred about being discharged and about her safety. She was interested in finding out what would be best for Mildred. Mildred was extremely fragile. She was emotional, withdrawn, and in need of care. Mildred looked at the social worker as if she were in a bubble trying to communicate. I told the social worker that she didn't have any money, any place to live, or any protection. I asked what she recommended. I didn't want to sound cynical, but I really wanted to know if there was anything that she could do. The social worker didn't have much at the time. She said she was going to make some phone calls and get back with us.

The next day when the social worker came back, she had some resources. She recommended putting Mildred in a shelter. They felt she would be safe, and could stay until she could afford to get a place. The shelter was located in Enumclaw, Washington. Enumclaw was a distance of about thirty or forty miles from Tacoma. The social worker had contacted them and they could take Mildred in. She also arranged for Mildred to have a police escort to the shelter. While I thought that was a good idea, I was quite skeptical, because Enumclaw was too far away for me in case of an emergency. Mildred did not have any money, and her mother needed care. I mentioned it and the social worker gave me a look as if to say I should be thankful for what she was offering. I was. She didn't know Mildred like I did. She didn't know that leaving Tacoma would devastate Mildred because she needed to look for her children here. Tacoma was the last place she had seen her children. What if they made it back and she was in Enumclaw, Washington.

I asked Mildred about her mother. She had not spoken to her that day. I suggested that she get on the phone to her sister so that she could come and get their mother. Suddenly, I jumped out of my chair. I startled Mildred. I said I know of a shelter here in Tacoma. It's a shelter for women and women with children. I actually sit on their board of directors. Why didn't I think of that before? Mrs. Mary East was the founder, and executive director of the Phoebe House Association; an emergency shelter and transitional housing for women and women with small children. I was so traumatized that I forgot that I sat on the board of one the finest emergency shelter and transitional homes for abused women in the state.

I told Mildred I would contact Mrs. East when I got home. It was evening and I would have to call Mrs. East at her home. Mildred looked at me with her big eyes, and managed to get a smile out. The smile got wider and wider. There was some hope for the seemingly hopeless.

Mary E. East and The Phoebe House

Mrs. Mary East was about 5'10" with a full figure. She was a strong African-American woman that had raised two children in Tacoma as a single mother. She was well educated, having attended college to receive a nursing degree. She became a registered nurse. She was a gentle giant in the community and was actively involved in ministry. She was a licensed missionary, and known to many in the spiritual community as Missionary East. Mrs. East cared for homeless seniors in her own home.

When I first met her, she was cooking full course meals in her kitchen and taking them to downtown Tacoma to feed the homeless. She didn't prepare just soup and sandwiches; she cooked chicken, vegetables, beans, corn bread, salad, and dessert. Mrs. East fed the homeless every week from the trunk of her car. Lines of people would form to eat her food. She would pray with them and tell them about the goodness of God. God was right there for them, manifesting in the aroma of her hot food and her generosity. Sometimes when the Holy Spirit moved upon her, she would sing a hymn. She had a melodic voice that could pierce through the coldest of hearts.

When I returned home, I immediately called Mrs. East. She was glad to hear from me. I told her I needed her help for my friend. I told her all the horrid details of Mildred's experiences. I continued to tell her about the missing children and the elderly mother. Mrs. East had seen many women and had heard many stories. She was intently listening to mine. She had spent many years of her life feeding the homeless and caring for the elderly, and now homeless women and their children. Her passion for helping women is a gift. Her clean and sober shelters have been home to many women in the Tacoma, community. I paused to get a response. She sighed. She said that both Phoebe Houses were full to capacity. My heart sank.

The Phoebe Houses can accommodate up to 36 women with small children. Not once did it occur to me that the Phoebe House would be full. I asked Mrs. East if she was sure. She said she would make a call and give me a call back. I prayed to God that something would be available. It was the perfect solution. The Phoebe House had an excellent transitional program. There was case management, assessments and counseling. They had programs that support self-sufficiency. They provided a myriad of resources and referrals to other social and community based organizations. They were the best advocates for women that I knew of. There was only one thing, Mrs. East ran a strict operation.

Her guidelines and policies were strictly enforced. She had that reputation and many court judges mandated women there on probation, as opposed to jail because of the strict policies and guidelines. The program was an 18-month program and most of the women stayed the entire time. There was always a waiting list to get into the Phoebe House. There really were no other programs in Tacoma that let you stay that long. If you were fortunate enough to get in there, you could finish your schooling and even go to college. I had known some that after leaving the Phoebe House, became independent and went on to get their bachelors and masters degrees. She conducted AA meetings and other drug and alcohol intervention counseling. She held Bible study every evening (spiritual enhancement) that was mandatory. Mrs. East would let you know about the God she served.

If you had children, you had to be responsible for your children. Those that were school age had to be enrolled in school. If you had classes or employment, you had to put them in day care. There was no babysitting aloud. Everyone had to prepare meals, and do chores. By 9 a.m., you were well into your routine. Everything in the homes was in good condition. They had formal dining rooms. Mrs. East would not allow junk of any kind. She would go through donations personally to make sure of that. She liked nice things and her houses had replicas of those things.

Most of all Mrs. East loved God. She founded the Phoebe House on Biblical principles. The name Phoebe came from the book of Romans when Jesus Christ acknowledged the help of a woman named Phoebe, because she was a helper of many. Mrs. East was a licensed missionary whose mission was to the needs of women in her own city.

Mrs. East finally called back. I held my breath. She said she could get Mildred in. I screamed in her ear. I thanked God! I thanked her; I knew she did some finagling to get her in. I was so excited. Mildred needed a breakthrough. If Mildred was going to be in a shelter, this was one of the best. It was centrally located in Tacoma. It was near the bus line and in close proximity to downtown, doctor's offices, and the courthouse. I could get to Mildred and she could get to me. I was so excited I could hardly sleep. I couldn't wait to get back to the hospital to give Mildred some good news for a change.

I got up early the next morning with halleluiah on my mind. I had to shout and tell God thank you. I took a shower and got dressed. I needed to get over there to catch the social worker. When I arrived she was there. She had arranged for the shelter in Enumclaw. I asked her if she had heard of the Phoebe House. She said she had. Well why in the heck would you want to send her to Enumclaw I thought in my mind. I informed her that the Phoebe House had an opening for Mildred. I gave the number to her so that she could call and make the arrangements. In the mean time, Mildred had made contact with her sister in Maryland. Her sister was getting a ticket to come to Tacoma and get Mrs. Olivia. There was only a week or so left before the eviction would be final. The optimistic look on Mildred's face was what I longed to see. She still had a long road to travel, but we were walking forward.

The social worker had coordinated Mildred's discharge from the hospital to the Phoebe House. It was going to be early evening. Mildred was extremely fearful. Her anxiety increased because she felt that John was going to be parked in a car somewhere watching her leave the hospital. Due to the threats, Mildred was going to wear a disguise when she left. She would not leave the hospital unless she was disguised. She was going to be picked up by the police and taken to the Phoebe House. She arrived at the Phoebe in late evening. The police car pulled to the rear of the house and Mildred was escorted in.

You can't imagine the relief I felt knowing she was safe. I went over to Mildred's house to check on her mother. I remembered driving around the block a few times to see if I was being followed. I don't know what I was thinking. I just wanted to be sure. John was out there somewhere. I knocked on the door and Mrs. Olivia opened it and let me in. I told her that Mildred was out of the hospital and in the Phoebe House. We sat down and I told her everything about the Phoebe House; that Mildred would be staying there for her own protection.

We weren't sure of John's whereabouts, but we knew he was out there somewhere. She told me that her daughter was coming and that she would be leaving to go stay with her. I told her that was the best idea. She needed support that Mildred could not give her at this time. She did not want to leave Mildred here, but she knew Mildred would not leave without the children. I asked her if she was fearful at the house. If so, I would contact the police so that they could watch the house. She adamantly said no. Mrs. Olivia just did not have that type of fear of evil. She said she had her God and that was all she needed. She relied on Him. Her voice was so strong and confident. I believe the God in her life was the same God in my life, so I did not fear either. God did not give us the spirit of fear, but of love and a sound mind. Mrs. Olivia's mind was sound!

I asked Mrs. Olivia if she needed anything. I looked around. I looked in the refrigerator. She had a few things. She wanted to go to the store. She gave me a list, along with some cash and I went to the store to get the items. I was back in about 30 minutes with her things. I took the groceries out of the bag for her and put them on the table. I reached in my purse to give the cash she gave me back. She moved my hand back. She would not take the money. I had paid for the food with my own money, and now she was making me keep hers. Mrs. Olivia was strong-willed like that. You couldn't make her do nothing she didn't want to do. She was not taking that money, her mind was made up! I leaned over and gave her a hug. We stood there and just held each other for a few moments. I told her that I would check in with her. I told her Mildred would be giving her a call from the Phoebe House in the morning.

The next morning I went straight to my office. I had not been in for two days. I checked my messages and returned some phone calls. I had already told some clients that I had a family emergency. The Phoebe House was one of my clients. I had a contract with the Association to provide accounting services. I did the work there in the accounting office. I went there later that afternoon. I went into Mrs. East's office. I had not thanked her in person for what she had done. I also needed to inform her about some other things that pertained to Mildred and her mother. She had spoken with Mildred and was aware of her elderly mother's situation.

I told her that Mrs. Olivia needed to see her daughter Mildred before she left with her other daughter for Maryland. Mrs. Olivia had not seen Mildred since the day the ambulance took her away from the home. Phoebe House had a 30-day 'block-out' policy, that did not allow outside contact with family and friends. During this time you were being assessed and getting your case management. Mrs. East made an exception in this case because of the circumstances. She always was conscientious of her client's need.

I went in to the caseworker's office. Doris was a good case manager. She enjoyed her job. Most of the women liked her a lot. She told me Mildred's room assignment, and I went upstairs to see how she was settling in. This was quite an environment for Mildred. She was in a shelter with women from various backgrounds. There were women there that were abused, getting out of jails and prisons, or with alcohol and drug addictions. Here she was a devout Muslim that did not drink, smoke, or eat pork. She was surrounded by women with many societal dysfunctions. She was a little concerned. I could sense her insecurity. I reiterated to her that the Phoebe House was a clean and sober transitional home.

All the women were trying to obtain some level of self-sufficiency. The women were in school, some were receiving legal help in getting their children back. Some were getting visitation with their children because they were in the Phoebe House. All the women had some type of personal plan to get their lives back together. I wanted her to know that she would be safe. I encouraged her to use the time at the Phoebe House to get healthy and to figure out what she wanted to do. She needed to get the legal resources so that she could evaluate her situation. I told her Mrs. East was going to allow her mother to come to the Phoebe House and visit with her before she left with her sister. She was also going to allow some of the women to help her pack and get her things out of the home. Mildred's situation began to take on a new course of direction, a course of stabilization and empowerment. These were the first steps of many toward getting healthy and some type of stability.

I went over to Mildred's house to get her mother. When I arrived, Mrs. Olivia was excited. I could hear it in her voice. She had been up most of the night baking and making homemade candy to bring to Mildred. She was finally going to be able to see and embrace her daughter. She did not waste any time getting her purse and exiting the front door. When we got there, Mildred had been waiting anxiously for our arrival. I showed Mrs. Olivia into the living room and there she saw her daughter. Their eyes lit up and they embraced each other. She handed Mildred the bag of goodies. Mildred gave me some of the goodies. Oh, they were good. I left them there to be alone. They had much to talk about.

I went back to the accounting office and did some much-needed work. Mrs. East came to the office to get a status on Mildred's mother and her arrangements to move. She had stopped in the living room and introduced herself to Mrs. Olivia. I told her that Mrs. Olivia was going to be leaving with her daughter; her daughter had purchased her ticket already and would be here the next day. I asked again if the rules could change so that Mildred would be able to spend time with her mother and sister before they left. Mrs. East agreed to allow them whatever time they needed. I gave Mrs. East a big hug. I knew that she had helped many women like Mildred and worse. I now had first hand experience of how valuable the Phoebe House and the work of Mrs. East are to women, their children, and to the whole community.

It was quite an emotional time for Mildred. Everything in her life was changing. Her life would never be the same. At least she felt that she and her mother were out of immediate danger. I had spoken over the phone to Mildred's sister. She was a Christian woman that had been praying fervently to the Lord for her sister, her nieces, nephew, and their mother. The communication had to come through me because Mildred did not have access to a telephone. Often I would let Mildred use the phone in the accounting office to call her sister. I cautioned Mildred that no one could know that I was giving her these privileges; it could start serious contentions with her and other residents. When Mildred called her sister, she did not hesitate to start preparing to come get their mother and do whatever Mildred felt was necessary. I was looking forward to meeting Mildred's sister. Mildred and I both were looking forward to her taking Mrs. Olivia back with her. We were waiting to exhale.

When her sister arrived, Mildred spent most of the day with her sister sharing the horrid details of the events that had taken place. She arrived with her husband and within 24 hours, they were on their way back to Maryland. A week had gone by since Mildred's family had left Tacoma. I knew that she had to be lonely without her mother. She now had no family in Tacoma; she was alone without her children or her mother. This was a vulnerable time for her, yet a courageous time.

I was the only person that she knew in the Phoebe House; the only one that she could trust. Our friendship turned more into family everyday. Our friendship increased through bonds of devotion to each other. We shared almost everything.Mildred was getting more in sync with her new living arrangements. She had thirty days of 'block-out'. She took each day at the Phoebe House one day at a time. The 'block-out' period was a critical component of the Phoebe House. Women needed to spend this time focusing on the matters before them. Mrs. East knew it would be easier for the women, if they didn't have any distractions or any negative influences. Mildred needed this time for herself; it was the first time that she did not have the responsibilities for her mother. She had only the responsibility for herself. The Phoebe House supported her in a way that she had not been supported before.

The doors were locked from the outside in. No one could get in, but you could go out. That was how Mrs. East designed it. Women could leave the program whenever they wanted. No one was forced to stay. Once you left, you would risk not getting back in. Your bed was usually given to the next person on the waiting list. Mildred was abiding by the Phoebe House guidelines. She was attending meetings and going to counseling. She was very polite to the women. She always replied "yes, ma'am" and "no, ma'am" to Mrs. East. She was doing her share of the work that had to be done in the home. She was preparing nutritional meals. She was a vegetarian and her meals were nutritious for every one. In her quiet time alone, she would pray and meditate. She listened to music by gospel artist Yolanda Adams.

Mildred was looking well on the outside. She had been getting some rest. She was now dressing in mainstream clothing. She had gone through the clothing closet and found some real nice garments. The Phoebe House had everything a woman in transition starting over and building a new way of life could need. Mildred's case manager was Doris Berry. Doris and Mildred hit it off real well. Doris was kind-hearted and very attentive to her clients.

She was one of the kinds of people who are just right for social work. The patience that she had was incredible. Doris conducted Mildred's assessment. Mildred had access to many types of resources now.

Mildred applied for public assistance. The Phoebe House required every client to apply. If awarded, a percentage of the money went to pay for your room and meals. If you were not eligible, you still received services. She was eligible for General Assistance Unemployment through the Department of Social and Health Services. The most you could receive was $339 per month. However, it was more than she had and it was coming in consistently. She received food stamps that she contributed to the Phoebe House to help with the food. This is the way communal living operated.

The Phoebe House corroborated with many other non-profit and community based organizations for services. One of the organizations was the YWCA. They had a shelter for women, legal assistance by attorneys and case management. One of the things Mildred needed to do was figure out what her legal rights were.

Mildred was exhausted, but she found the strength every day to start making some strides to getting information about her children. She was now out of the 30-day 'block-out' period. There was more flexibility with her schedule. She still had tremendous anxiety and fear of John ending her life. How was she going to face this Goliath? According to the authorities, John had all the power. He was the children's biological father. It didn't matter that she was their mother, and that the children had resided with her after John left the home. It didn't matter that she wanted her God given right to be a mother to them. The authorities said he had the right to take them away, at the expense of her right.

This seemed crazy to me. Why couldn't they find the children and let the family judicial system intervene. It doesn't matter if things had been vice versa. Each parent should be protected. If there is no custodial plan then a judge has to decide. Children should be placed in protective custody until the parents appear in court. A missing child is a missing child. There was a detective from the Tacoma Police Department that had been working with Mildred from the beginning. The FBI was contacted. Agent Shane from the FBI said that there was no proof that they were taken out of the country, so they would not get involved.

Months went by. The early months were difficult. Mildred continued to go out side disguised. She would not wear her traditional Muslim attire. If John's plans were to destroy her, she wasn't going to make it easy. She stayed in the Phoebe House away from doors and windows. John had many friends. He was the auto mechanic for most of the black people in the community. The word was out on the street that John had been asking people if they had seen Mildred. The problem that existed was that she had to go out into the public. The services that she needed required it. She had appointments with therapists and doctors. She attended domestic violence and abuse meetings at the YWCA. Boldly and bravely, Mildred went out each day taking every precaution imaginable.

When she would return, she would settle in and participate in the house activities. Mildred's smile and personality was contagious. She had made many new friends at the Phoebe House. I was amazed at how the women began to imitate her in certain ways. Some of the ways were in hygiene. She explained to them about the importance of proper under garments and coverings. She did not force any of her Islamic beliefs on anybody, however it sure did influence some. I saw women that didn't wear bras when they arrived at the Phoebe House, wearing bras and camisoles. Even some of the toughest, abrasive females eventually succumbed to her genuine smile and her kindness.

Mildred was small compared to most of the women. I would tease Mildred about some of them. She said her strategy was not to join them, but make them her allies. Allies is what they became, because the women had pulled together $200 of their own money to give to Mildred to hire a private investigator to try to find her children. Remember these are women with little money, living in a shelter and transitional home. That was an act of love.

One day I was working in the accounting office. Mildred knocked on the door. She had been waiting for me. She had a familiar look on her face, one that let me know she had a brilliant idea. She pulled out a piece of paper to show me. It was an advertisement of a paralegal home study course. She had clipped it out of a magazine. I read it and looked at her to see what she wanted me to do with it. She didn't understand why I wasn't excited. Sometimes I am so analytical, that I don't immediately notice simple things. Mildred drew my attention to the cost of the course. It was only $5. I now knew why she was so ecstatic. The course included divorce, child custody, collections, and a variety of other information. All of that, for $5. Yes indeed, it was not a typo or error. I checked. The only problem, Mildred didn't have $5.00. Well, all I had was $5 and I was hungry. It was my lunch money at stake. I gave it up and she took my $5 and went grinning out of my office.

Mildred had been volunteering at the YWCA in the legal department. It was a strategic move, because she was working on her divorce from John. She was putting the proper pieces in place to get her children back, but this time she was going to use the law to her advantage. About three weeks had gone by since the $5 episode. Mildred knocked on the office door and entered with a package. It was big and heavy. She had that familiar look on her face again. We opened the package and it was the paralegal course. What a course it was. It had a lot of stuff in it for $5. There were books, manuals, and tapes. It was a real home study course. I was in total shock that it only cost $5. God was in the blessing business and this was a big one. When Mildred left the office, she took her box and went straight to her room. She was like a child in a candy store.

Mildred was full of information; she was filing her divorce papers, child custody papers, and parenting papers. She had to run an ad in the newspaper announcing her intent to divorce. Apparently, this was how you file when you can't locate the spouse. She learned to write court pleadings. She went down to the county clerk's office and filed her papers. She had the attorneys at the YWCA look over her work. She filed a writ of habeas corpus, which was a document that mandated any law enforcement authority that found the children to extradite them to Tacoma.

Mildred was familiar with almost all the clerks. She knew some of them by their first names. She told them about her children being abducted. It had now been over one year and she had not seen John and their children. Over time, everyone that knew about her was assisting her and encouraging her to keep positive. Even the judges when she went before them to file her documents felt compassion and offered encouragement.

INPowerMent (In Power Me)

Mildred was known as Millie at the Phoebe House. She had been in the Phoebe House for about fifteen months. By then, she was being paid a stipend as Phoebe House staff. She worked the graveyard shift. This was a new position that was created at the Phoebe House as part of their employment readiness and on the job-training program. Mildred was a good worker. Her administrative skills were very good, and the Phoebe House benefited from them. Mrs. East was proud of Mildred. She had grown fond of her over the months. She had watched another women grow to become healthy and self-sufficient.

The only question was, where were her children? It seemed as if the children had vanished. Mildred had been optimistic, however, she was accepting the reality that she needed to go be with her family on the East Coast. She missed her mom. It was time to consider leaving Tacoma. Everything that she could do she had done. She was legally divorced and had sole custody of her children with permission to leave the state.

This had to be a difficult decision. It was something that would take much prayer and meditation. If it were me, I would have to hear God say, "Trust Me" and "I will never leave you, or forsake you. Trust that I will protect and provide for you and your children." Mildred was going to leave the last place where she saw her three children alive.

Everything was in order. She was not the same Mildred as before. She had more courage, more strength, and more determination to survive. She was going to be there when her children returned. She was going to be well and ready to take them into her arms. Mildred spoke with Mrs. East about her plans to go back east to Maryland. Mrs. East supported her decision. They developed an exit strategy that would get Mildred away from the Phoebe House, away from Tacoma, away from Washington.

The news of Mildred's departure spread throughout the Phoebe House. There was this stillness. Everyone wanted what was best for Mildred and wanted to witness the reuniting of her children to her. However, it just didn't happen. I was going to miss Mildred the most. I was going to miss my good friend. We had gone through some difficult times. However, I knew that being with her family would be best for her.

Now I would not have any diversion from the issues I faced daily in my own home life. I wanted to go back to southern California to be with my family. I was going through some unhappy times. My marriage was cracking. My abuse was not physical, it was psychological and emotional. My wounds were internal. I was hemorrhaging on the inside.

Mildred and I didn't discuss much of my perils. She knew that I loved my husband. It was easier for me to dive into her life than to deal with my own life. I had spent the last fifteen months not even focusing on how I was feeling about my life. I was facing the reality that she was moving on to grab her future and some how hold on to her past. My position as the accountant for the Phoebe House was not going to be the same without Mildred. Going there to work everyday afforded us the opportunity to comfort each other. We had some good times and we celebrated one another.

Mildred had made copies of all her court documents to leave with me and Mrs. East, so in case there was ever any breakthrough, we would have the proper documentation to get her children back. She left the address and telephone numbers to her sister's home in Maryland. She was now officially ready to go. Mildred left the Phoebe House and flew to Maryland. She telephoned me when she got settled to let me know that she had arrived safely. When I hung up the phone, tears came to my eyes. I didn't cry, but they were there.

Mildred continued to keep in touch with me. She kept her ears to the ground in Tacoma from Maryland. She informed me that she had found a job and was working. Her mother was no longer in Maryland, but in Texas, staying with her other sister. She had spoken to her mom and was planning a trip to go and visit. Mildred said Mrs. Olivia was doing fine. She was still the same, doing the same, but only in Texas. We laughed. Talking to Mildred was getting less frequent for the next few months. She was busy and I was now in my income tax preparation season.

John Allen Muhammad Speaks

It was on a Saturday that I was lounging around the house, when the telephone rang. When I said hello, a voice that I didn't recognize said, "Hello Sistah."

I responded in an obscure and curious voice, "Hello, who's calling please?"

He said, "This is John."

I paused in my mind thinking John? I replied, "John who?"

He said "John Muhammad. How are you, Sistah?"

I told him I was doing well. I really was in shock! I asked how he and the children were doing. I told him Mildred had been looking for him for months. Everyone has been looking for him, but had no way to reach him. I told him that Mildred had hired a private investigator to find him.

John laughed and said, "As you can see, I can be found if I want to be found. If I don't want to be found, no one is going to find me."

"May I ask why you disappeared?"

John laughed and said the children were fine and that they were in school. He ignored my question. He said they were active and taking swimming lessons. He said they were traveling and visiting places when they were not in school. John asked me if I knew where Mildred was. I told him I didn't have her address. After looking for him for over a year, she left and went to live with family. I said she was frightened of him and did not leave any contact information. I told him that she would contact me by email, and that was how we stayed in touch. I asked if he had her email address and suggested he try emailing her.

He said, "You know I don't do the computer thing."

I wanted to get as much information about John as I could. I wanted to keep him in conversation. I asked if he had a telephone number that I could give to her. He gave me a cell phone number. I wrote it down. It had a 206 area code prefix, so I asked if he was in Seattle or in town somewhere. He said he was, and he would keep in touch with me. He asked me to have her call him. He said that they needed to talk. He told me that the children missed their mother and wanted to talk to her. John said that he had to go and would call me back. He asked if I would try to reach her and let her know to contact him. He told me that I had always been a righteous sister and a good friend to them.

John's demeanor was calm and sincere. He spoke as if he had not done anything wrong. If I was not at the hospital that day when he called and threatened Mildred, I would have felt compassion. I would have believed him. However, I was there and I will never forget the look of horror on his wife's face. I will never forget the sound of her voice pleading with him to see her children. I emailed Mildred and told her that John had called me. I wrote:

"Yes Mildred, he called the house. I had just come back from San Diego when I got the call. We spoke for about an hour. He said hello, may I speak to Isa. So, I asked who was calling. He said John. I said John who? He laughed and said John Muhammad. I said who? He said John Muhammad and then he asked how many John Muhammad's do I know? I said this isn't funny, who are you? You know, John and Mildred! I said tell me something only you and I would know. He did and then he asked me where you were?

After I got over the initial shock, I had to calm myself to think what I should do and say. He stated that he needed to talk to you, that he hasn't seen you in over a year. YES, HE IS BITTER TOWARDS YOUR FRIEND OLIVIA! He said he was on the run from place to place, because Olivia had convinced you to call the police, the FBI, the Military Intelligence. He was calling me on a cell phone. He mentioned he was coming from Canada. (This may not be true.)

The only thing I wanted to do was to keep him talking, that's why I listened most of the time as he shared his version of the story. I mentioned that you had been sick, that your mom was in critical condition and living with other family members. He asked me if I had your number. I said no. Mildred, John seems to trust me. He feels that you and Olivia have 'poisoned everyone's mind towards him." I asked him what I could do to help. He gave me Olivia's phone number; he wants me to call her and ask if she would tell me where you are. I led John to believe that if Olivia would contact you about me, maybe you would call me. I told John I had not seen you in over a year. John would not give me a number to contact; he said only that he would call me again. I asked him what his goal is if I should hear from you. He said talk to her sister! You are the only one whose mind is not poisoned. I know she will listen to you. That I have always been righteous by you and him. YES, HE STILL THINKS YOU ARE MARRIED. I then asked again…John what is your goal? Do you want to see her? How can I help? I told him you are probably right, in that she would confide in me. He said Talibah just turned eight and she wanted to talk to her mom for her birthday, but he couldn't find you. He said Selena has braces. He said Lil John's forehead is at his chin. I told John that you are probably still in the area, that you wouldn't leave the area without the children. He agreed. He repeated, "Just talk to her sister." Mildred, I left a message with the private investigator again, right after I talked to John. I will call again tomorrow. MILDRED WE NEED A PLAN. Remember I said you may have to come and face John if you want to see your children. I want him to think that I have reached you and was able to get you to talk to me. I want to talk to the investigator before I, or we, get back to him. As long as he thinks I can find you, he will stay in touch. Mildred, I will be praying for God's direction and guidance in this. I don't want to do my will, but God's will. God is my defense and defender. I pray that God's Holy Spirit will provide insight into all the mysteries. I must hear from God before I talk to John again. If John sees me as a righteous sister, then I can only attribute that as testimony of God's spirit within me. All I want is to have you reunited with your children. I or we are ready to do this!!! YOU HAVE THE LAW ON YOUR SIDE."

"I LOVE YOU MILDRED."

Mildred didn't waste any time calling me back. She had so many questions. I didn't know where to begin. I told her again everything he said. I gave her the cell phone number that he had left with me. I asked her if she was prepared to come here to meet with him. Mildred was afraid to be with him because of the many threats. She knew he was capable of carrying out his threats. I asked what she wanted me to do. She decided to give the information to the detective that had worked on her case.

The next day I received a call from the detective. He said that he was going to run a check on the cell phone. I don't know if he did it or not. I no longer had any confidence in the Tacoma Police Department when it came to Mildred Muhammad. Since the hospital scene, John was supposed to have had a warrant out for his arrest. However, when Mildred volunteered with the Human Rights Domestic Violence office, she had found out that John had been stopped at different times for speeding, and the officer let him go. Was there a warrant in place? We had no idea. When the officer stopped John, he was not detained.

Trauma Of My Drama

Domestic abuse and domestic violence are so similar, but they are not the same. Both are deeply rooted with tentacles under the earth. You can have domestic abuse without the violence; but you cannot have domestic violence without the abuse. The abuse is the precipitation to the violence. Domestic violence is illegal. There is the physical manifestation of violence. It can be seen. Bruises are external and internal. They can be covered until it heals.

Domestic abuse is legal. Its bruises are internal with emotional and psychological damage. The wounds are deep and take longer to heal. Over time, you are hemorrhaging on the inside. No one can see it. I would get up and adorn myself in my professional clothing. My nails were manicured, my feet had a pedicure. I lived in a house and drove a decent car. I worshipped on Sundays. On the inside, I was bruised and hemorrhaging with the trauma of my drama. I didn't recognize the extent of it until after I woke up in the hospital from my first emotional breakdown. I don't even remember getting any therapy at the time. I just let time be my bandage.

The Tacoma community was desensitized to domestic abuse. Our local, state, federal agencies were desensitized to domestic abuse, as Mildred had contacted the authorities on every level regarding the threats on her life. She told them that John was a demolition expert and was capable of violence. Because there were no signs of violence, they just documented her statements and filed them. John had not physically abused her. Mildred dressed nice, hair done, nails, etc. No one could see the trauma from her drama.

John continued to call me from a 206 area code where he would say, "Isa, this is John, have you heard from Mildred?" I told him I had emailed her, but I had not received a response. I did email Mildred; she was not trying to be alone with John. She felt that he was going to destroy her. I reminded John of how fearful she was of him. She believed he was going to destroy her. Mildred told me not to give him her information. She wanted me to continue to get information to give to the detective. The detective also told me to contact him if I heard from John. That is what I did. John would tell me the children were fine. He said that Lil' John was going to flight school to learn to fly airplanes. He stated that they were living in Canada. Salena and Taalibah were growing and going to school. He said he promised them he would find their mother.

When John would call, I would always tell my husband Joseph. We didn't really think too much about it. I wanted to help Mildred get her children. It wasn't like we felt it was our responsibility, but we felt the authorities would handle it, once they found John and the children. I told John that Mildred and her mother had left Tacoma. I never told him where. I asked if he knew where her relatives lived and he replied no. John did not call in a few months. Maybe I watch too much crime drama on the television. I just knew that the police department had sophisticated technology. I just knew they were going to track him through the cell phone. They were going to track the sent or received calls on the phone. The 206 area code didn't reveal anything to the detective. I could only wonder if Mildred were white, would it have made a difference. Why was Mildred's case so unimportant? It had so little priority.

If domestic abuse does not take any priority, then this country will be in for some shame. The shame will come back to us if we don't do something. It will come back in ways we can't imagine. Who would have imagined Tacoma's own police Chief David Brame killing his wife and himself in front of their two children. Who would have imagined a decorated Army veteran John Allen Muhammad, with a child accomplice Lee Boyd Malvo, would become hunted killers for terrorizing the nation's capitol, the entire Washington, D.C. metropolitan area, and the entire country. The one thing in common in both cases is that both men were abusing their wives.

It was a beautiful day in Tacoma; we had our entire family over for barbecue. The Nichols family enjoyed barbecues and parties. We would make up any reason to have one. My husband was an excellent grill man. He would marinate ribs, chicken, and hot links in his own sauce over night. He would get up early at 7 a.m. and start preparing the barbecue grill on the patio. I would get up around 9 a.m. and start with the side dishes. I would prepare appetizers of divine eggs (I changed the name from deviled eggs), vegetable trays, and cheese and cracker trays. I would then start boiling some ham hocks for the greens. I would make my popular Isa beans and put the potatoes on for potato salad. We would then go and groom ourselves; by 2 p.m. we were ready for guest to arrive at 3 p.m. It was like clockwork.

That day, I got one more call from John from the same cell phone number. He said he wanted to check in with me; he wanted to know if Mildred had replied to my email. He said he was in the Bellevue, Washington area. Bellevue is about a 45 minute car ride from Tacoma. I asked him about the children. This time he did not tell me anything about his children. He ignored the question as if I hadn't asked. I didn't repeat the question. I just felt it was strange. I told John that I had to go because I had company. We hung up. I checked the caller ID and it was the same 206 number.

I went back outside to tell my husband that John called. He asked me what he wanted. I told him that it was the same questions about Mildred's whereabouts. Did you give him her number? No, Mildred doesn't want him to have it, I replied.

The doorbell rang. I assumed it is more invited guests. I looked out the window and it was John. I opened the door. He was there without his children. I was so shocked! I had not seen John in about two years. He was standing there with a wrinkled green suit, dark colored shirt, white athletic socks, and old brown penny loafer shoes. He looked like he was tired. He looked as though he had just crawled out of a bed with his clothes on.

"How you doing sistah," he replied as he smiled. I said I was well. I just stared at him for a few minutes while he was speaking. I remember looking in to his eyes. I didn't know where he came from because you can't get to my house in Tacoma from Bellevue, Washington in 15 minutes. I had just hung up the phone from him. I invited him inside. I wanted Joseph to see him. To see what I was looking at. He followed me to the deck where the family was. He said hello to all of the family. He gave my mother-in-law a hug. We were all surprised by his unannounced visit. We decided not to mention anything about Mildred and his children. Although we knew that he had abducted them, we did not know what to expect from him so we said nothing.

Joseph offered John a plate of food. He fixed him some BBQ chicken, greens, beans, and potato salad. I mentioned that the beans had pork; John ate it anyway. Muslims do not eat pork. John ate everything on his plate. He ate as if he had not had a meal in a while. Joseph and I looked at each other as he put down all the food. John finished eating and stated he had to leave. John and I walked to the front porch.

While on the porch, John talked about what led him to take his children. John looked directly into my eyes. John said he and Mildred had been separated, but he wanted to work things out. He said that he and Mildred had argued and separated before but would always consider their need for family; then they would work things out between them. He said that Olivia was influencing Mildred. He felt Olivia was against him. This was the first time that Mildred and he were not able to work things out on their own. John believed that if he could just talk with Mildred she would come back. He just needed to talk with his wife the way they had done in the past. John wanted me to tell Mildred that they could work things out.

I asked John why he took the children. His response was shocking. John used a metaphor of a burning house. He said Mildred was having telephone conversations with a man that she met over the Internet. He said he found out, by tape recording their telephone conversation. He said that all he could do was wonder if she had lost her mind. He felt that she could be talking to a pedophile and not know it. He felt that she was putting his children in danger. When he approached her about it, she didn't care. John felt that it was like his house was burning; when your house is burning you don't ask why, or any questions. You just get your loved ones out. You find out later what caused the fire. John said that his wife's behavior with the man she met on the Internet was dangerous and he wasn't going to stand by and wait for something to happen to his children. So he took them. Now he was ready to talk to Mildred, because he put the fire out.

I stood their looking into John's eyes. I didn't know what to do with the conversation. I was speechless. I had no response. I remembered what Mildred shared with me about the taped telephone conversation.

Joseph joined us on the front porch. We walked John to his car. John noticed that we had a white Nissan 300ZX parked in the driveway. He said that for a minute he thought it was his car. John and Mildred owned a white Nissan 300ZX with burgundy interior. He walked carefully around the car. He noticed that the only difference was his car had leather seats, and this one in the driveway had fabric. Joseph and I stood there while he studied the car. Now we knew why he stopped by. He saw the car. He thought Mildred was at our house. The Nissan 300ZX was too coincidental. He had to stop. Joseph and I did not own this car. It was on loan to Joseph from a friend of his named Sean. Joseph and I had been driving the car for a couple of months. Both of our vehicles were broken at the time. This was our only mode of transportation. I had not met Joseph's friend Sean. I assumed that Sean was a guy. It wasn't until later then I found out Sean was a female. I had been driving some female's car for months.

John left our home that day. He thanked us for the food. He encouraged us to help him find Mildred. He said he just wanted to talk to her. His children missed her and wanted to talk to their mother. He promised them he would find her. I told him when she would contact me I would tell her what he said. He said the cell phone number was still the same. I told John that the police were still looking for him and the children. His reply was not one of worry. He said as you know now, "I will be found when I want to be found. If I don't want to be found, I won't be."

John was driving a brown car. I had someone to write down the license plate number.

I emailed Mildred and told her about the unexpected drive by. I told her verbatim what had happened. I told her that she needed to make some decisions. I asked if she was prepared to face John. She was going to have to face John if she wanted to see her children. Mildred still felt frightened. She did not trust John. She felt he was going to trap her and try to harm her. Mildred said that she would not face John by herself. She felt she would face him only with police protection. She wasn't too confident with police protection. She felt that the police were no match for John Muhammad!

Mildred took the information and contacted the Tacoma Police Department. She contacted the detective that was assigned to her. She gave them all the information I had given her. The detective ran the license plate number for the car that John showed up in. The car belonged to Rebecca Beeler of Olympia, Washington. The police for the first time had a physical location to look into. For months, John had eluded the police in every effort they used to find him.

I knew Rebecca and her husband Walter. They once owned Your Fish House, a neighborhood eatery in Tacoma. They were once client's of mine. They owned the restaurant for a few years and eventually sold it to someone else. They were also Nation of Islam followers and worshipped at the same mosque with John and Mildred.

Mildred phoned me and said that the detectives were going to stake out the location of the address. They wanted to see if the children were there. Mildred had given them pictures of her children. Mildred was hopeful. She wanted nothing more than anything to find her children. Mildred was devastated to find out that Becky and Walter knew where John was all along. She remembered going to them and explaining to them how he had taken the children. She asked them to help her; to call her if they heard anything. She left them with information to get a hold of her. All those months and they said nothing.

Mildred's hope was diminished when the detectives went to the address and saw little children playing. The detectives claimed that when they approached the home, someone gathered the children and told them to run into the house. They did not know if the children were hers or not. The police were told that they had not seen John Muhammad. That was the last time that I had heard from John Muhammad. Mildred and I remained in touch occasionally. Things were pretty cold on finding the children. The police had not done very much. They were swamped with other cases. They had very little to do with Mildred and her missing children. I never gave up praying for their safety and for their return.

East Coast Bound

Mildred had lived at the Phoebe House transitional home for fifteen months, staying in the community in hopes of finding John and their children. Mildred's volunteer work at the YWCA's legal department rendered her valuable experience. Mildred had completed and filed her petition to divorce her husband John Allen Muhammad. In the petition, she had asked for sole custody of their three children. She had also petitioned for permission to leave the state of Washington with the children.

Mildred had taken control of her life. She became empowered by the same legal system that gave her minimal assistance and support when her children were taken. Mildred would speak with the attorney's at the YWCA that provided the pro bono work to its clients. She spoke with the law clerks and the court clerks. She would have them review drafts of her divorce filings. Mildred did not have a dime to her name: she did everything in longhand. When she took her paperwork to the courthouse, a clerk would make corrections. Then Mildred would redo the paper work. Mildred was at the courthouse often, speaking with whoever would give her information to assist her in the legal maze of filing for a divorce pro-se'. The courthouse staff was so accustomed to seeing her that they began to empathize with her. Mildred would share with them her story. They even knew her by her first name. They were in support of her journey to find her children. Even the judges that she appeared before wished her success in her journey to find her children. After posting her divorce filing in the newspaper for the required amount of days in hopes that John would respond; the judge granted her divorce. Not only did they grant her the divorce, but she was granted sole custody of her missing children. She was granted permission to leave the state. The dissolution of her marriage to John Allen Williams was the pivotal point of Mildred turning from victim to victory in her previous spiral of defeat, victimization, and despair. She went from powerless to empowering with the legal papers to back her up.

Although Mildred had this victory, she still did not have her children. The only thing she could do was to wait it out. She was hired by Phoebe House organization and moved into the transitional housing phase of the program. Phoebe House was staffed 24 hours a day. Mildred worked as the night staff member. Saving money was the goal. She had made up her mind to move to Maryland to be with her family. There was a need to be closer to her mother. Mildred gave Mrs. Mary East, Phoebe House's executive director, her notice to terminate her residency at the place she called home for fifteen months.

The news of Mildred's leaving the Phoebe House spread through the facility that housed eighteen women like wild fire. She had won the hearts of some of the most difficult population of residents at the house. They loved her. They had supported her the way that she had supported them. They were a family of women that had been abused and expelled from society. They prayed together, held each other, and supported each other during the hardest times of their lives. Mrs. East loved her clients.

However, there was something special about Mildred, whom they called Millie. Mildred represented the need for the existence of the Phoebe Houses. It was for this purpose the Phoebe House was there to help abused women and women with children to transition from homelessness, back into productive citizens in the community, to transition from brokenness to wholeness.

There was always hope that her children were going to be found. She had to believe that. I believed it, too. I was proud of her and I let her know it. When Mildred settled in Maryland, she called to let me know she had arrived safely. We spoke over the telephone often about her new life that she was making for her and the children. She had found a job and was saving money for obtaining more goals.

I was working in my office when Mrs. East buzzed me to come down to her office immediately. The tone in her voice was serious. She demanded that I stop whatever I was doing and get into her office quickly. My heart throbbed. At the Phoebe House, there were some real intense situations that would occur. Whatever it was, it had to do with me. What was the urgency I was hearing in her voice?

I sat down in a chair in front of Mrs. East's desk. She closed the door. I just stared at her looking for some sign for the mysteriousness. She sat at her desk and played a message over the speakerphone. It was a call from someone in Bellingham, Washington's Department of Social and Health Services. They were inquiring about Mildred Muhammad. I was confused. Mrs. East said that they were inquiring because a John Muhammad was applying for state aid for him and the children. Mrs. East returned the call the social worker at the Bellingham office. When John applied, the children's names were already in their system. Their address was the address to the Phoebe House. So the social worker was calling to verify some information.

I was now clear on what was going on. One of the Phoebe House's policies for its client's is to apply for state assistance. If they qualified, then a portion of their income would be used to help pay for their room and board. Mildred had applied in Tacoma and listed her children on the application. Mrs. East told the social worker that those children were the missing children that were abducted by their father. The social worker took down our information and said she would give us a call back.

When the social worker in Bellingham called back, she had contacted the Bellingham Police Department. She told us that someone from the Child Protective Services Department would be calling us. This was now going to be handled by her supervisor. Mrs. East and I thanked her. Little did this social worker know that she was about to unlock the chamber of horror for a grandmother, a mother, and a family that had been traumatized by John's decision to abduct his children.

Mrs. East and I sat in her office in shock. We were so hopeful that these were Mildred's children. We did not know how this was going to play out. Mrs. East and I held hands and we started praying. Praying was our routine at the Phoebe House. It was a house of prayer. We had to pray for funding, for the resources needed for the women, and often for the operations of the center. We prayed for Mildred. We prayed for the safety of her children. We prayed that God would restore these children to Mildred. We called on our Savior Lord Jesus Christ to restore, redeem, and deliver these children from any further hurt, harm, and danger. We cancelled, in the name of Jesus, any assignments that would stop these children from being traumatized any longer. The longer we prayed, the louder we prayed. We would take turns speaking to God calling on him to intervene. I was exhausted but I kept praying. I kneeled to the floor continuing to pray; speaking the words in the scriptures that would pierce through principalities and spiritual wickedness in high places. Mrs. East began praying in the spirit with the holy language of tongues. We both were speaking in tongues. An entire hour had gone by. We prayed until that phone rang and it was the detective from children's services.

The detective needed the information about the children. We faxed to him copies of Mildred's court documents and Mildred's telephone number in Maryland. We even gave the website address that Mildred had put on the internet. The website had pictures of the children on it. Mildred had developed this website in hopes that someone would have information to whereabouts of her missing children. The detective said that he would give us a call back.

Mrs. East called Mildred and told her about the telephone calls. She gave her the name of the detective for her to call. We were hopeful. Mildred had been praying for this day. I will never forget the melodic tone of hope in her voice. Mrs. East asked Mildred when and how she was going to get back here to Tacoma. Mildred had a friend that worked at a travel agency, who knew of Mildred's story, and who had told Mildred that she would be able to get her a flight out to Tacoma when and if she needed one. Mildred was preparing to see her children—John, Salena, and Taalibah. What did they look like? How had they changed? We would soon come to know the answers to all of these questions.

The detective telephoned back the next day. He had spoken with Mildred and was sure that these were her children. They were going to the address that John gave on the application. The detectives had told the social worker to continue to process the application for aid. They did not want John to get suspicious. The address that John had given was to a shelter in Bellingham, Washington. When the detectives arrived, John and the children were not there. The shelter director identified the children from a picture, however, they were using different names. He said that John was working and the children were attending a nearby school.

The detectives arrived at the elementary school and spoke with the school's administrator. The administrator identified the children from the picture; they were enrolled and in their classrooms. Again, they were under different names. The detective explained that the children had been abducted. The school administrator went to have the three children taken out of class and brought to the office. They called over the phone into each child's classroom and spoke with the teachers, apprising them of the situation. One by one, the children were brought into the office. It was over.

Mildred's missing children were taken into protective custody. They were immediately extradited.

Mildred received a telephone call from the detective. This was one of those true moments when your work rewards you in a profound way. The detective told Mildred that he had her children. For the first time in eighteen months, Mildred heard her children call her "mommy." That evening Mildred was on a flight to Tacoma, Washington. The travel agency came through with the ticket. She arrived in Tacoma in the morning.

I received a call from Mildred early in the morning. She was in Tacoma at the YWCA where she used to volunteer. It was great to hear her voice. The sound of joy from the anticipation of being reunited with her three children, John, Salena, and Taalibah, were only a few short hours away. We both could hardly contain our emotions. Was it really over? Was this season of mayhem finally over? Had God delivered us from this particular evil? The confirmation would be coming; Mildred said that she had to be in court at 9 a.m. Mildred asked if I would come to the courtroom with her. Without any hesitation, I said that I would. It was full circle; I had been with Mildred since the first day her children were taken by their dad. Now, I would be there when she would be reunited with them.

Eighteen Month Reunion

I arrived at the Tacoma Municipal Court House about 8:30 a.m. It was my plan to be there to support Mildred and to welcome her children. It was not my intention to see a family torn apart. I have always felt that the court would decide what was equitable regarding custodial issues for both John and Mildred. Now that the children were in protective custody, the court would establish a plan for the children. I had always felt that the authorities and courts should be the interveners when two parents are in disagreement and can't settle things between themselves. After a parent has reported that her children were missing, then the authorities must intervene and get that family into family court. It must never be at the decision of either parent. This is a vital and critical moment for intervention and prevention of lawful or unlawful children abductions.

When I cleared the security checkpoint, I saw Mildred in the foyer area. Our eyes locked and there was her beautiful smile. We embraced each other for a while. Mildred was trembling. I thought it was due to the emotion of being reunited with the children. Across the hall on a pay phone was John Muhammad. He was staring at Mildred and me. I looked at him to acknowledge him. He just gave a cold stare. The stare was not at me, it was at Mildred. Mildred ran. Her attorney caught her and immediately had her taken to the sheriff's office to wait until it was time for court. We found out that Mildred's court appearance was changed to 11 a.m., rather than at 9 a.m. With that news, anxiety overcame Mildred. She was still very fearful of John. Here we are in a heavily guarded courthouse and she was hysterically afraid. Then, I began to get a bit nervous.

We waited until 10:45 a.m. and we were escorted into the courtroom. There were other court cases being heard in court. When we walked into the court, John was sitting in a seat. We had to take a seat and wait for the case to be heard. To accommodate Mildred, the attorney arranged for us to sit in the front so that Mildred did not have to look at John. Mildred reached over and grabbed my hand. We squeezed each other's hand and then we just held hands until the judge called Mildred Muhammad vs. John Allen Muhammad.

Mildred and her attorney approached the judge. John approached the judge. He did not have an attorney. The judge looked over Mildred's file, which contained divorce papers and child custody papers. The judge carefully looked through the papers in the court file. He commented how everything was in order. There were no errors or omissions. Mildred had filed for her divorce pro-se'. All the documents were hand written. There was no sophisticated boiler plates used. She had filed every document with the courts. She had attended to every legal detail to divorce John Muhammad and to become the sole custodial parent for John, Salena, and Taalibah. She had also petitioned for permission to move and to leave the state of Washington with the children.

The judge looked at John and asked him if he had any questions. John's response was, "Your honor, why am I here?" John wanted the judge to explain to him why his children been taken from him.

The judge told John, "Mr. Muhammad, we are here to address the information in these documents."

John wanted to tell the judge his side of the story, but the judge would not allow him to address anything. It was not the purpose of the hearing. He told John he would have to get an attorney and schedule another court date. At that time, he would be able to address any of his concerns. This hearing was only to address the divorce and the returning of the children to the custody of their mother. The judge ruled in favor of Mildred Muhammad and ordered that the children be released immediately to Mildred. John stood there looking perplexed. He replied "So I, I don't get to see my children?"

The judge hit his gavel and rendered his decision. Mildred was now about to see her three children. Eighteen months had gone by since she had seen them, eighteen months since the day that she took them to school, only for them not to return home. Mildred turned to me as I left my seat to join her. We held each other. We cried with joy. John had left the courtroom. He never said a word. Within minutes, Mildred's attorney called child protective services informing them of the judge's decision, and that Mildred would be coming to pick up her children. While standing in the hall outside of the courtroom, I stood along the wall. I looked at Mildred and her eyes bugged out. She dropped everything in her hands and started running down the court hallway corridor. She just took off. I didn't see anything. I wondered where she was going. The attorney ran down the hall after her. I still didn't see anything. As I began to follow them both, John walked right passed me. He was walking rapidly toward Mildred. The look on his face was that of an angry man. I didn't know if he saw me or not.

John turned around and walked right past me again. I stared at him as he walked by. He didn't say anything to me or even acknowledge my presence. I turned and ran down the hall corridor to join Mildred. When I caught up with them, Mildred and I were escorted through a back corridor to exit the courthouse. When we came to the door there was a taxicab waiting. We entered the taxicab to take us to meet the children. I asked the cab driver to take me to my parked car. I felt that I needed to get my own car and meet up with Mildred. The attorney told the cab driver to drive around several different blocks before taking me to my car. After what we just experienced at the courthouse, she wanted to make sure that John was not following us. I didn't feel as if I was in any danger. Yet, I was going to be cautious. John knew where I lived. I felt he may come over to the house thinking that Mildred and the children would be there.

When I arrived at the Department of Social and Heath Services, Mildred and her attorney were standing outside in the parking lot. I parked my car and joined them. It was an extremely emotional moment. We waited for the children to be brought down to their mother. I wondered what they would say to their mother. What would Mildred say to them Mildred and I had talked about this moment along time ago. Now that day had come. The day when she would have to answer the many questions they would have. The day she would share with them how she felt without them. Share with them the many ways she tried to find them.

Suddenly the door opened, "Mommy", "Mommy." It was Taalibah. It was Salena. The girls ran to their mother. Mildred cried and smiled. They held each other. I couldn't move my feet. I just stood there full of emotion. My eyes watered at the sight of the love that was so pure. Lil' John came out of the office last. The children had grown so tall. They did not look like the children in their pictures that we posted everywhere. When they came out of the office, the girls were in pants. Their hair was not combed. They had on clothes that didn't fit. They were un-kept and looked neglected. They looked like children that lived on the streets; they looked like transients. John's hair was long. His clothes were old and dirty. He walked slowly to his mother. Mildred said, "Hello son." She held him in her arms. Lil John looked apprehensive; he didn't hold his mother like his sisters had. He was reserved. I knew that he felt betrayed in some way. There was no telling what he had been told. He was standing there looking confused, protective of his little sisters. As Mildred and her children got into the cab to leave, I told her to call me when they got settled.

I went back home to check on my daughter Tamara. I also called my husband Joseph. I shared with him the entire story. Joseph wanted me to go home in case John would come to the house. He did not want Tamara to be at home alone if he came there. I told him that I had thought the same way and was heading home.

When Tamara arrived home, I shared with her that Mildred had been reunited with her children. Tamara's response was joyful. She asked if we could go see them. She wanted to see that the children were okay. I told her that we could go when they got settled. Tamara wanted me to share every detail. I told her some parts, but not all of what happened. I wanted her to witness the answer to many prayers. I wanted her to witness how God is real and that we can depend on Him to deliver us from turbulent times. We talked about how good God had been to restore the children safely back to their mother.

Mildred and the children had gone to the Tacoma YWCA. When Tamara and I arrived, the children had been bathed. Mildred had selected some clean clothes from the Y's clothing closet. The girls were in nice dresses. Mildred had washed and combed their hair. Lil' John was dressed in some nice pants and a shirt. His entire disposition had changed. He was smiling.

They were glad to see us. I told Tamara to go hang out with the children. I wanted to talk with Mildred.

Mildred shared with me that she showed the children the website. She shared with them all here efforts to find them. They had been told that she did not want them anymore. That she didn't love their family. While getting them cleaned up she answered all their many questions. The children were really impressed with the website. It changed Lil' John's countenance towards his mother. He could see that she did try to find them. That with the World Wide Web she looked all over the world to find him. The children wanted to know so much. Mildred told them that they could ask her what ever they wanted. Mildred had always had a trust and bond with her children. She communicated with them just like she had before they were taken. Mildred said that they were leaving on a red eye flight that evening. I asked how she was going to get to the airport. She wasn't sure. A lot of things were being worked out. I gave her some spending money. It wasn't much, as I had stopped at nearby ATM before getting there. The YWCA was getting together funds to get plane tickets for her and the children to go back to Maryland. They were going to put them in a taxi. Somehow, this didn't set well with me. I wanted to take them. Mildred preferred to be driven as well. I asked Mildred if she had spoken with Mrs. East from the Phoebe House. She said she had meant to contact her, because she wanted Mrs. East to meet her children. I decided to give Mrs. East a call.

When Mrs. East answered her phone, I told her I was at the YWCA with Mildred. She was so happy for Mildred. I asked her if she would give them a ride to the airport that evening, so then she could see and meet Mildred's children. Without any hesitation she said she would give them a ride. I took Tamara back home and told my husband that Mrs. East and I were going to take Mildred and her children to the airport. Mrs. East arrived at 9 p.m. to pick me up. We then drove to the YWCA to get Mildred and the children. The YWCA staff was taking all the necessary precautions for Mildred's safety.

They had arranged for her to leave from a private entryway. Mrs. East and I pulled her car around to it and waited patiently for them to come out. Mrs. East hadn't considered the fact that John could be around following us until now. We had not considered that we could be in any kind of danger. What would we do if John showed up?

Finally, a door opened and out came Mildred and the children. They entered into Mrs. East's Cadillac. With apprehension, we quickly drove away. Mildred introduced each one of her children to Mrs. East. Mrs. East commented how beautiful they were and how intelligent they were. She told them that their mother loved them. She told them to take care of their mother. They replied, "Yes ma'am." When we arrived at the airport, I got out of the car with Mildred and the children. We went to the ticket counter. The YWCA had arranged for them to meet the airport police. When airport security arrived, they escorted Mildred and the children to a waiting lounge until it was time to board the plane. I stood in the middle of the airport and waived as they walked down the corridor with airport police. Afterwards, Mrs. East and I drove back to Tacoma.

The conversation we had in the car with the children answered some of our questions. The children shared some of their experiences. Taalibah shared a story of how she got into trouble because she had called her sister by her name Salena. They were not supposed to say their names any longer. She explained how her daddy got very mad when she called her sister Salena. Mrs. East marveled how bright and intelligent the children were. She hoped that Mildred would get them into counseling very soon. She had witnessed many times before homeless and abused women reunited with their children. This was another Phoebe House success story. Mrs. East had seen the end results of another woman that came out of brokenness and shame to her being healed, delivered, and set free. It was for this reason that GOD had called Mrs. East to be a missionary and to establish the Phoebe Houses.

Part Two – A Wilderness
The First Tragedy – The Untold Story

Keenya Cook was my 21-year-old niece. She was beautiful, in terms of physical attraction. She was a young mother with a six-month-old baby girl. She was a daughter, a granddaughter, a niece, a cousin, and a sister. On February 16, 2002, she opened the front door of my home near the Puyallup Indian Reservation at 2054 E 34th Street, Tacoma, Washington and was shot, brutally, in the face, with a .45 caliber semi-automatic handgun. The impact of the shot severed her spleen; rather I should say the bullet went through the lower part of her face and severed her spleen, causing her to bleed to death. My 14-year-old daughter, Tamara, found Keenya lying on the floor as she walked through the front door of the house to open the garage door.

Actually, I want to back up and start my story before that point. Before that moment, before that tragic day, Keenya had moved in with her Uncle Joseph Nichols, my husband, and I, so that she could get away from her physically and verbally abusive relationship with her daughter's father. Prior to allowing Keenya to stay with us, we met over dinner to discuss Keenya's goals, what she wanted to accomplish in life, and to see if we could help her meet her goals. We agreed that Keenya's goals were obtainable and allowed Keenya to move in to our home with the baby.

Keenya was getting her life back on track. Keenya worked very hard on her job as a retail assistant manager at a women's clothing store. She later left her job to go on maternity leave, and then after giving birth she decided to go back to school. Keenya had applied for housing assistance, and completed all the tedious paperwork involved in obtaining the various types of financial aid available to low-income single mothers. She would come home every day, where she had the folders of paperwork needed to get housing and medical assistance, and to enroll in classes. Her interest was in restaurant management. She liked to cook, and she could cook well. Aside from all this, Keenya was a new mom and taking care of Angeleah, her baby girl, which she enjoyed most of all.

It was really a joy to watch Keenya and the baby bond, in the safety of our home away from the baby's abusive father. I felt good about being able to experience her giving love and nurturing this beautiful new life in our family. To be able to watch Keenya be the best mother that she could be was a great reward. She was willing to make whatever change she needed so that her baby would have a better quality life. So, I watched her proceed with her life: making the necessary changes in her life to start being independent, to heal her own feelings from abuse and neglect, and to replace those with love, self-esteem, and education. Our decision to allow her and the baby to stay in our home meant that we were allowing God to use our blessings to bless her and them. That's what Keenya was to me, a blessing.

The morning of February 16, 2002, I remember waking up to the telephone's ringing. It was my husband Joseph Nichols telling me that he and his brother had arrived safely in California. They were on their way to a friend's house, and I can recall telling Joseph to call me when he got settled.

He said, "Okay."

I said, "I love you and be safe."

He replied, "I love you too."

I laid back down because I had made up my mind that I was going to take some time to sleep in and just get the rest that my body needed. So, once I knew Joseph was safe in California and everybody else was out doing his or her normal Saturday routines, I laid in bed until approximately 1:30 or 2 p.m. After a good rest, I got up, made a nice hot cup of coffee, and made a couple of telephone calls.

It was tax season and I was preparing taxes for clients from my home office. One of my clients came over for their annual appointment. Most of my clients have been clients for a few years, so our professional relationship automatically turned into friendship very easily. By having my practice at my home, it made for a friendlier environment, as I could offer my clients a beverage or a snack while I went through their tax information. It was also great because my male clients could watch sports on the television, while their wives would be doing the tax work with me.

At about 3 p.m., shortly after my clients left, Keenya arrived with the baby and we decided to go to the grocery store. One of the agreements that we had with Keenya is that she would buy food as her contribution to the household. We didn't charge Keenya any rent or for utilities. She would just contribute groceries. On this particular day Keenya, the baby, and I went to the Safeway grocery store. We had a blast of fun because the baby was catching all the attention from everybody that walked by our cart. The baby was cooing, laughing at people, and giving them big smiles. What would normally take 30 minutes to shop turned into an hour and a half, because of all the attention the baby received.

We also stopped to get something to drink on the way home. There, Keenya and I began to dialogue. Keenya shared with me how she had a wonderful weekend with the baby's father. It was Valentine's Day; he had given her a flower and some Mylar balloons. They got along that weekend and she was feeling good about that. I was silent because I wanted to just listen as she shared with me. I wanted to keep my opinion and judgment to myself. I begin to shift the conversation to our living arrangement, our agreement. I wanted to check in with her to see how she was doing with her goals, her finances, and her budget. I just wanted to make sure that she was still on task with what she wanted to accomplish and to see if she need anything from me. I asked Keenya if she was going to go back to the relationship. She was hesitant and replied "no."

We talked about our arrangement and how it was allowing her to save her money so when the time came she could get an apartment, furnish it and be able to pay for utilities, etc. There was just a very warm feeling in my heart as she explained to me what she had accomplished. We drove back home and brought the groceries into the house.

Keenya asked me if I would fix some chicken tacos. Chicken tacos are a very popular meal and a favorite that I often would cook for my family. It was requested at least once a week. I told Keenya, sure, I would cook, but as we were putting up the groceries, I noticed I didn't have any taco shells. We hadn't bought any taco shells. I told Keenya I would go back to the store later and get some taco shells. We put up the groceries, and I went back to working on my client's taxes. Keenya went upstairs to begin changing her baby.

I remember the doorbell rang. Keenya's mom and her best friend came by. They were on their way to attend the Bill Cosby concert. Keenya's mother was an avid Bill Cosby fanatic. She had wanted to attend the concert, but no one really wanted to go with her. Finally, her best friend had purchased some tickets, and they dressed up, planned to have dinner, and see Mr. Bill Cosby. Keenya laughed, as her mother looked incredible that day. She just flounced around to every mirror in the house with her new outfit. She was so happy. She was going to see Bill Cosby! She wanted to borrow binoculars to see the show. She wasn't sure where she was sitting and didn't want to miss anything. Keenya complimented on how beautiful her mother looked. She kissed her mom and told her to have fun at the concert. Her mother went whisking out the door, looking glamorous. That was her nickname to most of her nieces and nephews – Auntie Glamorous.

Shortly thereafter, I received a telephone call. It was my 14-year-old daughter, Tamara. She was talking to Keenya. Tamara had asked what we were doing and Keenya told her that we were going to make chicken tacos for dinner. Tamara insisted that we not make the chicken tacos, since she was not home. Tamara was supposed to be at a sleep over, and all of a sudden, she had changed her mind and wanted to come home. I told Keenya to tell her that I would pick her up on my way to the store to pick up the taco shells, and to be ready because I was going to honk the car horn.

I left shortly thereafter and grabbed my keys. I went to go get Tamara and go to the store to get taco shells and a few other things. I closed the door. Then I went back into the house to get the frozen chicken out of the freezer. I saw Keenya in the kitchen, and I asked her to get the frozen chicken breasts out and boil them so that when I returned, the meat would be ready. She said, "Okay, Auntie." Then I left, and closed and locked the door again. I got in the car and commenced to go pick up Tamara.

I stopped at Safeway, and then I remembered that I needed to get some information from a friend, who was a softball player acquaintance. There was a softball tournament in Las Vegas coming up. I had played with this Co-ed softball tournament team for a few years, so I stopped by there to get the tournament information for the February tournament. It was a treat to go Las Vegas because the weather was warm in February, unlike the wet climate in the Northwest.

Keenya Cook, shown here with her baby, was shot to death February 16
AP Photo

The weather was a bit cloudy, and it was almost dark. Tamara and I were driving up the street towards our house. We pulled into the driveway, and I told Tamara to go into the house and open the garage door because, I was going to put the car into the garage for the evening. As I sat there, listening to the local jazz station, I was wondering what was taking Tamara so long to open the garage door. Tamara can be easily distracted. I began to get a little anxious because she should have had the door open by then.

I looked up and Tamara had come back out to the car and stood there with the most disarming look of shock on her face. As I stared at her, I could see something was wrong with my child.

I got out of the car and I asked, "Tamara, what is it? Why haven't you opened the door?" She just stared at me.

I kept asking, "Tamara, what is it?" As I got out of the car to come close to her, she finally spoke and said, "The house is all smokey and Keenya is lying on the floor."

I turned off the engine, took the keys, and went to the front door. There as Tamara had said, was Keenya lying in the doorway, with her feet at the front door and the rest of her body lying in the foyer of the house.

As I looked into the house, there was a pot on the stove. The electric coil burner on the stove was orange. The smoke was at the top of the house. You could feel the heat from the kitchen from the stove burning. My first thought was that Keenya had succumbed to smoke inhalation. I ran into the kitchen and somehow was able to get the stove turned off, and I tried to remove the pot; however, the pot had melted onto the burner of the stove. But, I did turn the stove off.

I went back to Keenya. I kneeled over her body and grabbed her hand. I called out her name repeatedly. Keenya's eyes were open, glazed and fixed. They was just a blank, glazed stare. Her hands were cold and stiff. There was a small hole in her face, under her eye on the cheek. At this time, it really hadn't registered that she had been shot. The thought of Angeleah crossed my mind. I ran upstairs because I thought that the smoke might have affected the baby. This was not for real! This could not be happening!

Finally, I saw a small casing, a little metal casing next to Keenya's head, and I realized this was not smoke inhalation, that something was terribly wrong with Keenya. I saw the little metal piece, but I didn't touch it. I immediately ran to the phone to dial 911. I was praying so hard. I felt so helpless.

I cried out, "Lord, Lord Jesus, help us!" I prayed that Keenya would hang on. I remember screaming to her, "Hang on, hang on Keenya! Keenya, Auntie is here!"

Within minutes after talking to the operator, I could hear sirens far off in the distance. It was then that I ran upstairs and I saw the baby. I was so very fearful because the baby was lying on her stomach and was not moving. I didn't know whether or not if something had happened to the baby. So I touched her back, and she jumped up and started screaming and crying. The baby was naked, and had rolled her way to the edge of the bed. Near the bed, there was a change of pajamas, fresh unused diaper, and bottle of warm milk. As I grabbed the baby and held her, the baby just grabbed my shirt, screaming and yelling. I grabbed the towel, the blanket, and wrapped the baby up, and she began to calm down. I did not know how long the baby had been lying there, but apparently, the baby had cried herself to sleep when her mom had not returned.

I came downstairs. I handed the baby to Tamara who was standing on the front porch in the same position she was in when I left her. Tamara was in shock. She had not moved the whole time. She would not come into the house. She could not speak. So, I handed her the baby on the front porch to hold. It never occurred to me that someone could still be in the house, but I could still hear sirens coming closer. I turned to Tamara and I told her to take the baby and go to our neighbor's, our friend's house. Tamara left with the baby. I told her to go and call her grandmother.

Finally, the paramedics arrived and the fire department arrived too. They came in and they saw Keenya lying there. They pulled Keenya from the foyer into the living room in order to get enough space to try to revive her. They put oxygen and tubes down her throat to try to get her to breathe. They checked her pulse, but Keenya was already dead. I had knelt down and held Keenya's hand. There was no life. They covered her up with a white sheet. I stood there, staring in disbelief. This just could not be happening. Keenya was gone.

The First Murder Scene

When the police arrived, they made me leave the house. They began to secure the house in case there was evidence. They would not allow me to go back into the house, because they were looking to see if there was any evidence to figure out what had happened. The police and the fire department called their chaplains, who had come and tried to console me. It was a Saturday night, and most of the detectives and coroners were off duty. They were being called at their homes regarding this crime. That was the explanation to me for having to wait. But while I waited, I couldn't go in the house to get clothes; I couldn't get shoes; I couldn't get my coat; I couldn't get my purse; I couldn't get the baby's things. I couldn't get anything because the house was officially a crime scene.

They began to put yellow tape across my door and a police officer guarded the door, waiting for other law enforcement professionals to arrive. I just walked back and forth on the sidewalk in front of my front door. The door was still open. I just looked and stared. Then, neighbors came outside their homes and cars began to slow down. The police began to redirect traffic, to block off the intersection near my house. I just paced, waiting for detectives and coroners to arrive. They could not remove Keenya's body from the house until the coroner arrived.

In a few hours the coroner finally arrived, they removed Keenya from the house and put her lifeless body in the ambulance, where she remained until the rest of the investigators got there.

My neighbor, Mr. Aho, was the father of Tamara's best friend, Tanya. Tamara showed up at his home as I had asked her to. He told me that Tamara and the baby were at his house with his daughter Tanya and his wife. He told me they were ok. As he came to the house, I had to tell the police that he was my neighbor, and that I needed his help. Mr. Aho pulled his van in front of my house, and allowed me to sit in it, out of the cold, until law enforcement officers began to arrive. Hours went by before I could go anywhere. I was alone, and it was still not registering that my niece had been shot and killed.

I just sat in shock in Mr. Aho's van watching more and more law enforcement personnel's arriving. Finally, familiar faces arrived. It was friends of the family. They had just received word from my mother-in-law that Keenya had been hurt. They came as quickly as they could. The police allowed them to come and talk with me, and I told them that Keenya had been shot. They cried in disbelief. They were in shock. I just stared at them. It was as if I could see them crying but I could not hear them. There was nothing I could say to them. I didn't have any answers. I didn't know how, what, why, or anything.

I was approached by the fire chaplain and was told that they wanted me to sit in the detective's car. I told them that I could not go anywhere without my daughter, who was at a neighbor's house. Mr. Aho went and got Tamara and the baby. When Tamara and the baby arrived, they got into the detective's car with me. The Aho's had gone to the store and bought some formula and some diapers for the baby. Tamara held the baby, who was asleep in her arms. I put my arms around them both. We were so pitiful. We waited in the detective's car for almost another hour.

Finally, they took us down to the police station. We went down to the police station and went up to their conference room area to wait for further questioning. The police were trying to make us comfortable, offering us coffee and water. We sat there, Tamara and me, staring at each other. The baby had woken up and was looking around to make sure that we were still there. It was obvious the baby was still traumatized. Tamara had told me she had contacted her grandmother and had told her that Keenya had been shot. She began to cry. I was just numb. I kept trying to console my daughter, but no words would come.

The detective came in and began to question Tamara and I about what happened. We explained to him how we had arrived and found her. He began to ask us if we knew who could have done this. We both replied, "No!" They began to ask us about family members and their whereabouts. We told the detectives that my husband was in California and that we had not made contact with him. I had not spoken with him since about 9 a.m. We also told him of Keenya's boyfriend, the baby's father, and where he lived, and gave the detective his name. We gave them Keenya's mother's name and information. We just answered all of their questions regarding individuals and whoever may have known Keenya or who Keenya may have talked to or contacted that day.

When we mentioned Keenya's boyfriend's name, the detective went to another room and when he returned he showed us a picture. He asked us was that her boyfriend. Tamara had identified him by saying, "Yes." They informed us that he was a gang member.

I didn't know much about Keenya's boy friend, other than Keenya had met him in high school, when she was about 16. He was much older, around 8 years older; too old to be with a 16 year old. Keenya moved in with him shortly after she turned 18. The police said that he was a thug, and that he belonged to one of the local gangs. I knew that he had hit Keenya many times before and that he was very abusive to Keenya. I also knew she was afraid of what he would do. It was a very volatile relationship.

I remember the night we moved Keenya's belongings from their apartment. We were very nervous. We were afraid of what he would do if he came home and saw us moving Keenya's belongings out of his apartment. I remember seeing empty cans of Old English 800 Malt Liquor. Cans were everywhere. I remember seeing some brass knuckles on the table. The urgency was clear to me when we moved Keenya's belongings.

When the officer brought out his mug shot and rap sheet, I was surprised. Just like I said, I didn't know very much about the baby's father, but I became very fearful because I couldn't imagine him doing something like murdering Keenya. It was just incomprehensible. This was his baby's mother. Then the detective left us in the room again.

My cell phone rang and it was my husband, Joseph. I finally broke down and began to cry. I was quite relieved to hear his voice over the telephone. I needed him so much. I was so alone. I didn't want to let him go. I figured someone had called him in California and told him about Keenya. I remember asking him to catch a flight to Tacoma, because I didn't want him driving from California knowing the shocking news of Keenya being killed. He sighed and replied that he would be here, that he was on his way. I took that as he was going to drive anyway or that he was going to find a way to get here. I told him that Tamara and I were okay and that we were at the police station, all he said was, "Isa, I'm on my way!"

I didn't want to let him off the phone. I just needed to hear his voice. I wanted him there so badly. I felt that if he was there with me, somehow I was going to be alright. Tamara and I needed him.

Tamara and I just sat there, making the baby comfortable, still in shock at where we were and why we were there. Suddenly, someone knocked on the door and grabbed the doorknob, and it was my husband Joseph coming through the door. He was there with his brother. All I could do was to stare at him, like I had just seen a ghost. I was so confused because I had just talked to him; I thought he was in California and there he was, within minutes, walking through the door of the Police Station in Tacoma, Washington. I was so confused that I just sat there and stared, almost like I didn't know him. He went over to Tamara, and held his child, and then the baby. I literally could not move. I just stared at them.

I can't tell you what was going through my mind. I was traumatized. I was devastated. It seemed just like the utility company shutting the power off at your house. I had just shut down. I became mute. I then realized that I was in real trouble. Something was terribly wrong. This was going to get worse before it could ever get better.

The detectives came back in the room, looking to see who these men were. I told them it was my husband Joseph and his brother, Keenya's uncle.

The detective was looking quite puzzled because Tamara and I had just told them Joseph, my husband and her father, was in California. He didn't say anything, just shook their hands, and asked them if they wanted anything, water or coffee, and then he let them sit down. They had apparently been to the house, and saw the house – and realized that we were no longer there. They were told that they could find us at the police station. I don't believe they saw Keenya's body. When we left for the police station, Keenya was covered up in an ambulance. I don't know if she had been taken away from the house at that time or not. I can only imagine what it was like for Joseph to come to his home and to see it taped off like a murder crime scene. I can only imagine what it was like for Joseph to wonder what could have possibly happened. What occurred at his home?

Numb

We were finally allowed to leave the police station. Since our house was now an official murder scene and we could no longer go in it, we went to my mother-in-law's home. Family members were all crying. Tamara was still focused on taking care of baby Angeleah. I recall at that time still being in a daze. I tried to explain to Joseph's family the best way I could, but I couldn't process any more. Tamara had shared with them the details of what happened over the phone. That could probably be why no one had questions of me. No one asked me any questions.

We realized that Keenya's mother was still at the Bill Cosby concert. How were we going to notify her of Keenya's tragedy? We were all worried about Keenya's mother getting the news over the television, because this was a breaking news story, and reporters were still filming the house constantly. We were worried that she would get news of this somehow before we could get word to her. At some point, she was reached and the news of the shooting re-quired her to be taken to the hospital. I know she was in the hospital much of the early morning on Sunday, February 17th, and then they released her.

I stayed at my mother-in-law's house for two days while we notified family members and relatives. We notified Keenya's other grandmother who raised her in the Maryland-Washington, D.C. area before she came to Washington. I contacted my family in San Diego, California. My family felt helpless and in despair. They were fearful that I was in danger,

There were so many phone calls to make, but the ultimate call was to one of my professional associates in the Pacific Northwest Chapter National Black Chamber of Commerce. Zane Fitch owned a mortuary. I contacted the mortuary to be prepared to get Keenya's body released from the coroner.

Zane Fitch returned my call within minutes. He told me not to worry, that he knew what to do. It had been a while since I had been back to my house. It was days before we were allowed to go back into the house.

Joseph and I eventually went back to our house. There was blood; Keenya's blood stains in the foyer entry and on the living room carpet where they had pulled her when they were trying to revive her. There were splashes of her blood on the walls. I began to remember in my mind the images of finding Keenya the night of the murder. The house still had the awful stench of smoke. The house was pretty much ruined from the smoke smell from the burned stove. When I looked into the pot, the chicken that Keenya was boiling had just disintegrated, and the pot had melted and was stuck to the stove. There was yellow tape around the doorway and markings on the floor. Several detectives were talking to neighbors, canvassing the property, the grounds, and the alleys looking for clues, looking for information that could be helpful in trying to determine what had happened at my house.

There were so many messages left on the phone from family, friends, reporters. There was a knock on the door; some more detectives had come by the house. I opened the door and I let them in. They were quite professional and as I hung up the phone, they were waiting to ask us some more questions. They informed us that they had not been successful in finding Keenya's boyfriend. They had been out to his house, and asked if we knew of any other place we could find him. My husband and I didn't know anything else to tell them.

The telephone rang and it was the baby's father. He said, "Hello, is Keenya there?" I looked at Joseph and said he is asking to speak to Keenya.

I said,we have been looking for you. Everyone has been looking for you. Keenya has been shot." I didn't tell him Keenya was dead. He said that he was on his way to our house.

The detectives immediately notified the police to move their cars, and I began to look at my husband with nervousness, we just didn't know what to expect. The detectives said that they would just wait, but they radioed for everyone to clear the street, so as not to draw attention that something was wrong or cause DeAngelo not to come to our house. The detectives and officers positioned nearby prepared for his arrival.

Keenya's boyfriend arrived with his friend. He immediately looked down and saw the blood on the floor, and grabbed his head with both of his hands. As he came into the kitchen area, the detectives stepped up.

He asked, "What happened?" The detectives informed him that they wanted to speak with him. He was surprised, wondering what happened. How did this happen? He wanted to know what happened; he wanted the officers to tell him what was going on. The detectives put him in handcuffs and took him down to the station.

Joseph commented to him that we all had been questioned, that we all had been down to the police station. I was so nervous because I just didn't know him and the fact that someone would murder Keenya left me just wondering, "Are we still in danger?" Wondering what could Keenya possibly have done to anyone that they would want to kill her? The fact that the detectives had showed us Keenya's boyfriend mug shot and said that he was a member of the neighborhood Crips gang, just left a very horrid feeling in my stomach at the possibility of Keenya's murder being gang related.

While we were still at the house, I began to wonder and ask myself, "How in the heck am I going to clean up this house?" Keenya's blood was everywhere. I asked the female detective, "How do you clean up stuff like this?" She went to the patrol car and gave me a business card of a company named Bio-Clean that could assist in cleaning up my home. She told me that they were very good and police departments used them to clean murder scenes frequently. I took the business card and stuck it in my pocket. I was quite relieved that there was a resource to clean up my home.

The events of the day were quite overwhelming, so I just put the card in my pocket for a later day when I would be ready to deal with cleaning. I knew that some day I would have to deal with getting the house cleaned up. We headed back to my mother in-law's house. Joseph shared with them that the police had taken Keenya's boyfriend into custody. I checked in with my baby girl Tamara. Tamara was still taking care of baby Angeleah. She would not leave her alone. She was quiet most of the time, but I felt that her taking care of the baby was consoling her in some way. I felt that they were actually consoling each other. Most of the family members were now at my mother-in-law's house, and it was becoming very crowded, because it was only a 2-bedroom apartment, and some eight people were all there.

Joseph shared what happened at the house with Keenya's boyfriend. .Keenya's mother and everyone around us expressed the feeling that Keenya's boyfriend could be responsible for Keenya's death. Keenya's mom couldn't imagine him killing her child. The pain and the shock of this entire ordeal was just beginning to settle in on us. Despair and grief were imminent in everyone.

The Fourth Day After the Murder:

It's now February 20th, the fourth day after the murder; when I got a call from the police. They wanted to talk with Joseph, Tamara, and myself for more questioning down at the police station. We went back down there. They took Tamara to a room, and we waited outside. I noticed that we now had new detectives in charge of the case. They introduced themselves and told us that they would be working on Keenya's case from that point on. It was two white male cops, a Detective Webb and another whose name slips me. Eventually it was my turn to go in and the detectives began to interrogate me. They began to ask me questions to tell them again what happened. They were particularly interested in my husband's whereabouts on the night of Keenya's murder. I told them that I thought he was in California and I found out that night that he had not gone to California.

Of course, they had a field day with asking me, why my husband would lie. Why he would tell you he was in one place when he was in another. I had no explanation. I told them they should ask him that question, that he would be better suited to answer it, because I just didn't know. Joseph is a liar, but that doesn't make him a killer.

All I knew was that Joseph and his brother had left for a short vacation for the weekend, a short getaway. All I know is that he called me that morning and said that he had arrived safely in California and would call me back when he got settled. The detectives felt that something was terribly wrong and that there may be a reason that someone was there to kill me instead of Keenya. The detectives asked me if I was aware that an insurance policy had been taken out on me just prior to the murder? I told them I was aware of one policy and it was a policy that we had for 20 years. It was a term insurance policy that we had gotten right after we had our first child and that policy was still in force. I looked at them and I asked them whom the policy was with? They told me that they could not release that information because of the on-going investigation.

The interrogation room was similar to the cop shows, like one of the Law and Order police drama shows. There was a long conference table where I was sitting in one chair and the two white male police officers sat across the table from me. One would ask questions, while the other would observe my expressions. Then the other would ask questions, while the other would analyze. They took turns. I kept feeling like they were trying to make up a story, rather than allowing me to tell the story. Their line of questioning was very personal in nature, but I had nothing to hide.

The detectives began to play good cop, bad cop. The good cop would be very consoling and understanding, and then the bad cop would be hard and make it plain that they were going to find out exactly who killed Keenya, and that they did not give a !&$# about any of us. After the bad cop said that, I took offense and reminded him that I pay property taxes that pay his salary and that his job was to find Keenya's killer. And if it meant he needed to start with the investigation of my personal life, then he needed to just get it over with.

Once again, I reiterated I had nothing to hide. They continued to question me about whether or not my husband was having an affair, so I admitted that he had affairs before. They wanted to know if I felt that he was having an affair the night Keenya was killed. I told them I wasn't sure that he could have, and that I did not know his whereabouts and, again, that was a question they should ask him. Then the nice cop reassured me of the roles of responsibility they had because they see this type of stuff everyday. They had to be this way. Regardless of the harshness and tone of their voice, they were there to do their job in finding Keenya's killer. Once again, I agreed that I too wanted them to do their job.

Then they asked me one of the most appalling questions ever, did I think my husband was sleeping with Keenya? With that, I had enough! Of course, they looked at my every expression and my reaction. My response was no, I didn't feel that my husband was sleeping with Keenya! I didn't feel that my husband would do anything like that, anything of that nature with his niece. They asked me how I could be sure, how could I say that. In my mind, I really had no way of being absolutely sure as they put it; but I didn't want to think of the fact that Joseph could have been sleeping with Keenya. I felt like I was going to vomit.

The detectives continued to dwell on the fact of my apparent failing marriage and they began to pressure me into thinking that this could be the cause of Keenya's death. The murderer was really coming after me and that this was a case of mistaken identity.

When I left the station, after three and a half hours of constant questioning that basically defamed my character, opened up areas in my marriage that were old wounds, areas in my marriage that although were shattered and fragile, now were apparently broken. I really did not understand why Joseph would lie. I didn't understand what reason he would have for being in one place and telling me something else. Often in our relationship when he went out, he would just not come home. When he came home, he would make up some story that he was with his brother or hanging out with the 'fellas'. We would engage in an argument. I never liked it or appreciated it when he would leave and not come home. He would not call to say he was okay or that he wasn't coming home. I would be up all night worried, angry, and sometimes crying.

The detectives had asked me if Joseph had affairs before and I told them yes. They asked me why I would stay. How could I stay married to a liar and a cheater? He said that his wife would not tolerate that type of behavior. I told him that's why she is his wife, and I am Joseph's wife. I said I have a gift to forgive. I forgave and we went on with our lives. They asked me how many affairs that he had that I was aware of. I told them several.

"Are you that naive?" I said no! I had known about some of his affairs. There were probably some that I didn't know of. Being a soldier in the military on deployment from your family would make it impossible for me to know what he would be doing.

Detective Webb asked how many affairs I had had. Joseph and I had separated in 1992, I saw another person casually during the separation. I dated for companionship, but it would not last. My companions felt I would not leave my husband. They knew I was emotionally connected to Joseph.

I could never get over the love I have for my husband. He is the love of my life. We both had seen other people during our separation. In 1999, we reconciled and I had no other relationships after our reconciliation. The names Cecil, Stanley, and Tony came up. The police asked if they were lovers of mine and what they represented in my life?

Cecil is a good friend of my father, me, and of my entire family. I explained that we were close, as he would help me with my disabled father. As a friend, I cared about him. I explained that these people were friends and business associates of mine. Tony was my business partner of seven years. We were Nichols, Wright, and Associates. It was apparent to me that the detectives had been questioning other family members and these names were given to them.

The detectives returned the questioning to my faltering marriage. I couldn't help sometimes thinking of the possibility that some woman would want to kill me so that she could have access to my husband. Joseph had returned to his patterns of being gone all night. That's like something you would see on television. The detectives let me know that the things that we see on television are the things they see in their line of work everyday. They said all of the questions that they asked me pertaining to the insurance policy being taken out on me, to my husband's infidelities, to our finances, were all motives that they had seen for murder, in their combined 50 years of police work.

Joseph was in the lobby and we all went back over to his mother's house. Tamara went back into the house while Joseph and I just sat there outside in the car talking quietly. I'm so confused. I tried to look at his eyes to see if I could see anything that would cause him to be connected to this in any kind of way, if my life was really in danger, if somehow, someone could really be planning something that was meant for me. Could it be a fatal attraction from one of his affairs? As I stared into Joseph's eyes, I could see hurt. I could see guilt and I could see pain. I could see anger. I wondered what he saw when he looked back into my eyes. I felt fear, betrayal, and anger. I felt alone and abandoned. I wondered if he could see any of those things when he looked in my eyes. Amazingly, I still felt love for him. Joseph and I, we just had very few words to say. I just had no words to even start the communication between us. The communication that was really needed. So, I remained silent. And he did the same.

Keenya's Funeral:

We returned to my house that afternoon. It was time to make funeral arrangements. Keenya's body was finally going to be released to the funeral home. I had contacted Destiny Center Ministries, the church that I attended, and St. John Baptist Church, the church where my father was a deacon. I had already contacted a good friend, Zane Fitch, the funeral director and owner of the Upper Room. It was a family business. I had attended funeral services for people that he had provided services to and I felt that he did very good work. It also helped that the fact that he was a friend. We would see each other from time to time at different networking events in the community.

When I placed the call to Mr. Fitch, he wasn't there. He called me back within minutes. He handled all the arrangements with the coroner for getting the body released. He also was informed that we didn't have any money to bury Keenya. I told him that I had resources that I was looking into that would pay for Keenya's services. When I mentioned it, he was familiar with the one I had chosen. It was called Victims of Violent Crime organization. There's a process you go through and Keenya qualified to receive victim's compensation funding that would pay for the funeral. Mr. Fitch had worked with this organization before and he was able to get the paperwork started once I gave him a case number. He explained to me how they worked and that they would pay him for his services. He was just awesome.

I notified the family and we began to work with Mr. Fitch on Keenya's funeral. Victims of Violent Crime is a nonprofit organization that provides a variety of services to any victim, whether it is a survivor or the victim itself.

Some of those services include counseling, financial support, burial assistance, and advocacy. I had contacted the local chapter for Pierce County, Washington and was asked for the police case number; after which I was given a claim number. Once I got the claim number, I gave it to Zane Fitch, who was now able to handle the funeral arrangements.

What Zane Fitch did for our family was really incredible. Because he was in charge of the funeral directing, he could wait for his payment, but the cemetery had to be paid in advance of Keenya's burial. Mr. Fitch wrote the cemetery a check for me. For this I am so grateful. Although we were still obligated to reimburse the mortuary for payment, we were compiling our resources to get the funds together. Friends and people that heard of the tragedy began to give money to help cover expenses.

Zane's assistance was very much appreciated by me. I realized that he had written off a lot of extras and put in a lot of extra work that he had not billed us for. He even went so far as to include an extra limousine so that the entire family could have transportation for the funeral. He was quite consoling, yet very professional, as to the trauma and the toll of the tragedy on me personally. I really appreciated the work and the support that he provided to me and to the family in the time of our immediate bereavement and need.

The funeral arrangements kept me quite busy. I was not able to touch the surface of the shock of how tragic my life was at that time. I wanted the funeral to somehow be a gift to the family of how sad and apologetic I was that this happened to Keenya in my home. I wanted the funeral services to be a celebration of love, because Keenya was loved. I wanted the funeral to be a memorial of how beautiful and how special she was to me and to our family. I wanted to disassociate Keenya's funeral from the horror of what happened to her, the tragedy of her death, and somehow try to find the peace and grace that she was now with the Savior, that she was resting. Making the funeral arrangements were a solstice for me. I gave a lot of updates back to the family on the funeral arrangements, being very careful to get what they wanted. It was so very painful for everyone.

Keenya's mother was just reeking with pain, in tears and fears for what had happened to her child, her baby. Keenya was her youngest child, her baby girl, and then having to look at little Angeleah, her 6-month-old granddaughter, made it more horrific. We actually had to watch the 6-month-old baby grieve. At the mention of her mother's name, she would look around. You could see on her face as she was so diligently looking for her mother to appear.

Every time someone said Keenya around the baby, she would stop whatever she was doing, and look to see if it was her mommy. Sometimes I wondered if Keenya's spirit was around, because sometimes it felt like there was her presence in the room. I never said anything about feeling this presence of energy in the room, but I definitely paid close attention to the baby's constant motion of looking into open space, looking up as if someone was standing beside her. Then she would start crying. That was unbelievable to me. Other people began to notice that the baby would look around and stare at a location or a space in the room and start crying. I remember getting the baby and holding her, and she stared at me. I looked into her little eyes and she actually put her arm around my neck. I began to hold her like I used to do everyday in her life that she was with me. As I walked around the room, she just laid her head on my shoulder. I began to pat her softly on her shoulder, and she began to pat me on mine.

One of the things that I decided to do was to design and to write Keenya's obituary. I wanted to make Keenya's obituary something the baby would have some day when she was old enough to read. I wanted it to be a keepsake to send to everyone who loved Keenya, to see what a gift she was and the perfect gift she left with us, Angeleah. Angeleah was so special to me because Keenya added Leah to her name. Leah is my middle name. I wanted baby Angeleah to one day be able to read and know how wonderful and beautiful her mother was, and how much we all loved her and her mother.

I started the obituary with the sunrise of Keenya being born, the first day she was taken home and put into her older sister's arms to hold. There was a snapshot that I had found of baby Keenya, a few days old, in the arms of her six-year-old sister. I used that picture to introduce Keenya on one cover of the obituary. In the center of the obituary, I used a picture of Angeleah by herself. Underneath the picture of Angeleah was a poem. The poem would be a poem from Keenya to Angeleah. I started to write one evening, when the baby was on my heart. I began to start writing and all of a sudden, all of this built-up emotion filled within me and tears had clouded my eyes, that I couldn't finish the poem.

I called a friend of mine who was a poet. I used to be a mistress of ceremony at poetry slams, which are poet competitions. I read to my poet friend what I wrote and I sent it to him. I sent it to him so that he could see what I wrote. I told him how I really had to say this, because I didn't have a way to really let the baby know about her mom. I wanted to finish it but the tears, it was so painful that the tears were in my way. So he, along with another poet and friend, finished the poem for me.

It's entitled "The Mother's Song of Angeleah."

Baby, cry if you must...

But don't cry long.

My song is sung beside you

In a forever chorus –

A force to guide you

Through these loving days,

To comfort and protect you

As you grow and play.

In my autumn way

I am lifting you gently

I am the wind in your spring

I will sing you back
Into summer's warmth
And lay with you into the safe
Hearth of returning winters.
For no one knows the hour
No one knows the time
When they will be called
To be with the most high ...
The divine
We find strength in things not seen
We hope of things to come...knowing
That there's a place waiting for us
In the everlasting kingdom.
Settle into rest,
My tender Angeleah;
Nestle into love,
My gentle Angeleah.
When the branch flickers
In the steady wind,
It is me,
When the rain dances
Down your path,
When the sun soaks
Your soulful hair,
Your mother is in the air.
So fear not my precious
Angeleah, (for) I have gone nowhere,
For as long as you live...So too do I.
My song – it lives inside you...
A mother's lullaby.

The third picture was a photo of Keenya smiling, hair down her back. Underneath Keenya's photo was the story telling about her life, telling about her life with her new baby. Then I talked about Keenya's sunset, the day of her passing. I used a picture which resembled how she appeared most of the time. She was beautiful, charismatic. Then on the back, I was thinking about what I could say about Keenya, I led off with a scripture from the Book of James, chapter 1, verse 17. "Every good and perfect gift is from above, coming down from the Father of the heavenly lights…."

As I began to reminiscence that Keenya actually was a gift to every individual who shared in her life, I wanted others to realize that Keenya was leaving us a special gift of joy and love, that being her six month old daughter, Angeleah Ashanti Yves Rogers.

The fourth and final picture was one we had just taken four months ago around Thanksgiving with the entire family, the last picture that we had taken as a family, prior to Keenya's murder. I used that picture on the final page of the obituary. I did the acknowledgement of condolences, special thanks to different people, and thanks to people that helped us during our time of grief. I remember thanking friends like Candace, Jean, and Addie. I remember thanking the management staff of Fashion Bug, the store where Keenya worked. I remember thanking the poets, Lucas and Paul. I remember thanking Robin Henderson, my friend at Key Bank for setting up a contribution trust fund account for Keenya's baby. I remember thanking Destiny Center Ministries.

I remember thanking St. John Baptist Church, John Leach, and Laser Writing. John Leach was the man that put the obituary together; he was the typesetter and printer. His work was just outstanding. He actually did the brochures in 11x16 and all in color at a very low price. You could tell he put his compassion for my family's loss into his work. I remember thanking Zane Fitch, the Upper Room Mortuary, and Mountain View Cemetery. I remember thanking Carrie from Victims of Violent Crime. I remember thanking the

Tacoma Police Department and the Tacoma Fire Department for their assistance the day Keenya was murdered.

After I thanked all these individuals in writing on behalf of the family of Keenya Cook, it was really my prayer that the Lord would bless each and every one of them and that He would keep them, and that the Lord would make His face shine on each and every one of them and be gracious to them, and that the Lord would turn His face toward them and give them all peace.

The obituary was to be my atonement for the tragedy that took place at my home. It was interesting, because before the final printing of the obituary, I had made sure that I had all the input from the Nichols' family. We had the obituary being read by me. We had the musical selections by Keenya's aunt and her very best friend from high school. We had the acknowledgements and remarks by another aunt. We had both pastors – one from my current church and from the church that I attended for six years. I provided a draft of the obituary to the family to look at and to read.

They commented how beautiful it was and that they appreciated my efforts. I looked at their faces. Another prayer came to my mind. I remember getting into some place quiet and writing the prayer down. As a final remark, I stood up at the funeral and I read this prayer. It was a prayer request for the family called "The Power of Prayer."

> *The power of prayer, that prayer from the righteous availeth much. Prayer can change things, and prayer can enter into places no one else can go. I said that when you pray for a family, I ask for people to pray on these things: that no weapon formed against us would prosper; that GOD would set free, heal, and deliver each of us; that the Lord is the strength of our life; that the GOD of our Lord Jesus Christ, the Father of Glory, gives to each of us the spirit of wisdom, and revelation in the knowledge of HIM; that GOD would continue to bless each of us and to keep us. I asked that people pray for the husbands in*

our family; that they would love themselves, therefore loving their wives more than themselves. I asked people to pray that the men in our family would stand and be the men of GOD according to their purpose. I asked people to pray for the wives of our family, that we would be the helpmeet that GOD ordained for our husbands. I asked people to pray that we would be submissive unto our husbands. I asked that people pray that the covenant that GOD joined for our marriages, that no man or woman could put asunder. I asked the people at the funeral to pray for the single women in our family, that GOD loving, spirit-filled men would come into their lives, and that, until such a time, that they remain in close relationship with GOD, our Father. I asked everyone at the funeral to pray for our children, that grace and mercy would be forever with them, that they be raised up to be obedient, to honor their parents, so that their days would be long on the earth. I asked the people at the funeral that they would pray that we would find peace that our family would find love, and joy, that our family will rejoice in the Lord always.

So many people wanted to know what they could do for me. All I could come up with was prayer. I needed prayer. I was raised in a house of prayer. My daddy and mama always prayed, no matter what happened. So prayer was what we did in impossible times. The whole entire family needed prayer!

As the procession for the final viewing of Keenya's body began, it was the final goodbye to a beautiful young woman. Those in attendance slowly walked single file in procession around her casket. One by one, friends walked slowly to pay their respect to Keenya and the family. Once everyone had proceeded out of the church; the door was closed and it was time for the family to say good-bye. It was now the end of the public viewing recession, and now time for the family viewing. It was quite difficult because she lay there looking so innocent. When I walked up to the casket, I looked down at her for the final time. I had seen her when she lay on the floor in my home. I had seen her when she arrived at the mortuary from the coroner. I was there when her body was being dressed for her services. I took a deep breath and released it. I looked down at her beautiful face, I closed my eyes. I dropped to the floor.

Keenya's boyfriend's mother, grandfather, and sister were in attendance. They were in remorse. They genuinely loved Keenya and the baby. Keenya's boyfriend's mother repeatedly cried out that her son did not do this, that her son did not do this. The police detained him at the station for parole violation and therefore was not in attendance at the funeral. I can imagine the pain at the fact that this had happened, and that her son at the time was the police's number one suspect.

Keenya was now being removed from the church. The Nichols family was consoling one another. We had to go to the cemetery. It was the usual Northwest rain outside. We rode in the limousines through the neighborhood along with a procession of cars. I was so exhausted, I sat in the car during the burial. I was feeling euphoric and dizzy. I watched from the limousine window. my niece preparing to go into a grave.

We returned to the church for the repast with family and friends. During the repast, there were many people there to console the family. There were people who presented sympathy cards with cash; I wanted people to remember that we had set up a contributions trust fund account at Key Bank for donations to take care of Angeleah. This little baby would grow up without her mother and not really knowing the fate of her father.

The media was in frenzy. They literally camped outside of our front door for three weeks. We were the breaking news story in the Tacoma-Seattle area for two weeks as police continued to find and look for clues and updates on the mysterious murder of Keenya Cook. I remember literally praying because of all of the hurt, the rumors, the gossip, and speculation that was going around. The media was at the funeral, as well as the Tacoma Police

Department detectives looking at the rawest of emotions from different people in attendance.

Friends and Community

I felt that a trust fund account in the baby's name, with her uncle Joseph as the executor, would help provide money to send the baby to college some day. One of my clients and friend, Robin Henderson. was a banking officer at Key Bank. She set up the account so that anyone could go into any Key Bank and make a contribution into that account. We had this information to give to any and everybody in hopes that the media would broadcast the information on the airways as they were covering the story, so that our community could do something incredible, or do something on behalf of this beautiful baby that was left here. It was also an opportunity for the community to support that this baby, that she would have access to a decent life as she grows up without her mother. Well, I gave this information to the local news media.

I gave an interview on the auspices of their using the story of what happened and announce the trust information over the media for anyone that may want to help. But unbeknownst to me, the media said very little about the trust account, and deliberately used the interview to gain listeners for their purposes. It was apparent that they were only interested in selling the sensation of the story, more interested in telling the story of the murder and how we were dealing with the tragedy.

Keenya's murder was a continuous media frenzy for several weeks. All five networks had production vehicles on all four corners of the house, waiting to talk to anyone, mainly myself. After my experience with the reporter who I allowed to do an interview with me in hopes that he would inform people of the trust account, I no longer trusted the media, because they used so little information about the baby's trust account. I just didn't trust the media any more. I knew they were just out to sell their news. From that point on I stayed away from them. However, I was the only one who felt that way because the Nichols family appeared many times in the paper.

The media was consistently capturing their rawest feelings of hurt, and now anger and confusion. It was all over the news. There was so much speculation as to who could have committed this crime and the media was hanging onto every thread of dialogue, every word that they could pick up on for the story. The police had assigned a public relations person from their department to give media updates. However, the investigation was really just beginning.

The police were canvassing and reinterviewing witnesses. As they were taking these statements, and as bits and pieces of information was getting into the press, the press would contact members of the family. Whoever would open their mouths to talk to them regarding the information they had, would be published in the paper or broadcast. At that time I really had no clue as to who could have done this to my niece. The police investigation was not going well at all, because they were focusing on Joseph and me.

Eventually, Keenya's boyfriend was released from custody. He had been rigorously interrogated and given a lie detector test and he passed it. The detectives told me they were pretty sure that he had not committed the murder. The investigators continued to pursue their thoughts of someone coming for me. They also questioned whether my daughter was involved in any gang activities or had any enemies. They were convinced, I won't say convinced, they were making assumptions, that this was retaliation of some sort, some retaliation or mistaken identity.

Life Interrupted and Homeless

During that time, my home was still in a crime scene shamble. I had left my mother-in-law's house and accepted an invitation from my dearest friend, Linda Braddy, to live in her home. She had not attended the funeral. I accepted the offer and moved in with her. As I started the process of repairing my house, I found the business card of the company that the detective had referred to me that could clean up the blood and possible contaminations. I had also contacted them to see how to start that process, and they immediately returned my call and met me at my home.

I went to the house alone that particular evening to meet with them. I had circled the block to see if there were any reporters parked nearby. I went into the house after seeing that there weren't any reporters. I pulled the car into the garage and waited for the clean-up people to arrive. They were on a ferry and would not be able to get to Tacoma from a previous methamphetamine lab that they had cleaned up.

When they arrived, I was surprised to see two white females owned this business. They were very professional and very compassionate. They came in and I was so glad to see them. It seemed like they had done this before. They made it known to me that they had performed the clean up for the Nicole Simpson and Ron Goldman crime scene in Brentwood, California. That right there let me know that they were the experts in the field.

I sat on the staircase, two steps above where Keenya's head laid, while I allowed them to come in and assess the clean up that needed to be done. They entered in and put on overalls and gloves. They had different types of tools and supplies. I remember asking one of them if I needed to be covered up, and their reply was only if I wanted to help them do the cleaning.

I laughed and kindly said, "Thank you, but no. No, thank you." As I stood there, I watched them remove every plank up from the hardwood floors one by one. When they picked up the plank, it had been at least three weeks since Keenya's murder, and the plank from the hardwood floor was still moist and saturated with blood.

The blood had penetrated and had actually bled down almost two feet to the foyer of the hallway where Keenya laid, from where her head was. Each plank that they pulled up was saturated with Keenya's blood. It was truly apparent that she had bled to death. Here I was, thinking that the blood was only going to be in the area where her head laid. I was so shocked that the blood had traveled so far, and that the 26 planks of wood which they took up, were each saturated with her blood. They took all those wood planks up until you could see the concrete slab of the floor, upon which they sprayed on a solution. Then they cut around the bloodied area of the carpet, basically in the shape of where Keenya's body laid.

The blood came to be in the carpet when the paramedics moved her from the original location, into the living room where they tried to revive her. They cut that carpet until you could see the concrete on the floor and then they sprayed it with more of this special decontaminating solution. They explained to me that blood is so contaminating, that Keenya could have had an infectious disease and not been aware that she was infected, and that the contamination of blood would still be in carpet fibers, wood planks and walls. The solution they used was a solution that killed bacteria and prevented the spread of contamination. They then began to spray the walls and ceiling. They saw blood splatters that I had never even noticed.

I thought to myself about my first instinct, which was to get a carpet cleaner and get a mop, and just mop the floors myself. Boy, was I naïve. This was actually a job for professionals. There was no way I could have cleaned the house properly. I sat there on the staircase and watched them clean, then began asking them questions about their line of work, because I found that this was kind of interesting. I found them interesting, because not only did they clean crime scenes, but they were also called quite a bit to clean all kinds of contaminations. Their plate was full with cleaning methamphetamine labs in the Pierce County, Washington area because of the highly toxic chemicals and contamination that the chemicals leave in making methamphetamines. They shared with me that cleaning methamphetamine labs in a building structure, whether they are homes or not, have to be gutted out completely. The entire place has to be gutted out in order to get rid of those types of contaminants. They cleaned my house for almost three hours.

There was a knock at the door. It was a friend, Leroy, who had just stopped by on the way home, when he saw a light on. I opened the door and he came in while they were still cleaning the house. We sat on the stairway and had conversation. He wanted to let me know that I was in his prayers and he wanted to see if there was anything that I needed. I said that I could use a shot of brandy. He said he'd be right back. He came back and knocked on the door with a small pint of brandy. We poured a glass and we sat on the stairway while the cleaning team continued to clean the house.

We marveled at how this could have happened to Keenya. He also wanted to know if there was anything the police had come up with. I basically said no, and that the only suspects they had were members of the immediate family, and Keenya's boyfriend. Of course his reaction was that he was appalled when I said I was a suspect, and the rest of the family members are suspects. But, in reality, who knows? I certainly, after being interrogated and some of everything thrown in my face, really didn't know anymore. All I know is that this beautiful 21-year-old young woman had been murdered in my home.

The cleaning team finished and, although the house was clean, there still was much work to be done. The next day I was contacted by our State Farm Insurance Company. Reggie Johnson, our insurance agent, came and gave condolences because they had seen the house on the news. Immediately my insurance agent recognized that we were his clients. When he arrived, he was compassionate, and wanted to do whatever he could to make things on the insurance side of things clear and simple. The insurance company gave us a list of contractors that they dealt with that were licensed and bonded to perform the work. I gave that information to Joseph so he could contact them and make that decision. All we had to do was pay the deductible and they started right away.

They replaced the kitchen appliances. They relayered the hardwood floors. They put in new carpet. They cleaned and had the vents cleaned of smoke. They replaced furniture that was damaged with blood spots. We had white living room furniture. They paid for all of the clothing in the house to get dry cleaned, as the stench of smoke was in all of our clothing. They also paid to have the furniture professionally cleaned to see if the blood stains would come out, but they were unsuccessful; those blood stains wouldn't come out. They ended up giving us money to replace the furniture. The insurance company gave us a check based on the replacement cost of the furniture and the appliances we had that were replaced. Joseph and I used the money to try to rebuild our home. I found out later that his family wanted to know where we were getting money from. They thought we took a policy out on Keenya. Can you believe that?

We were able to order a garage door opener and a new screen door with locks. We wondered if we had such things, could this have prevented the tragedy of when Keenya opened the door. Somehow I thought that, if there was a storm door between her and the person on the porch, would she possibly still be alive? I remember driving around the neighborhood, and my friend Linda's neighborhood, when I noticed that many of the front doors had no screen doors either. Some doors had storm doors, but most doors had no screen or storm doors. It's funny how I would start thinking about ways that could have possibly saved Keenya's life.

We also used our monies to try to make our home more secure by putting in a light sensor and a video camera that would allow us to see who was at the door before going to the door. We weren't doing this because this was something we had always done. We were doing this so we could increase our security when we moved back into our home. We still did not know who killed Keenya. I realized that our sense of security would never, never be the same, that our ability to feel secure would just not be the same. It took almost 45 days before the contractor completed the renovation on the damages.

A Friend Indeed To A Friend In Need

In the meantime, I took solitude at Linda's home. Linda lived on the north end of Tacoma. It was a comfortable, split-level home with all the amenities of a warm home, a normal functioning home. There was exercise equipment. There was healthy food. There were vitamins. There were televisions, stereos, and a fireplace. It was the perfect place to be still and start to figure out how to begin to heal. Linda holds a special place in my heart.

She left on a trip to Las Vegas, Nevada for the softball tournament that we played in every year. I had airlines tickets to go also. But before Linda had left, she had come to the funeral home with me when Keenya's body was released. Linda's coming there, while I was the only other one there to view Keenya's body was God's timing. Linda and I viewed Keenya's body together, and we held hands and we prayed. Shortly thereafter the mortuary staff began to prep Keenya for the funeral. Linda then left for the airport for the trip to Vegas; the trip that I should have been on, playing softball with my team. She was a great friend! Stepping in, I had no idea I had people in my life that were so caring, awesome. God literally put wings on Linda that day because I had no one there for me. Not anyone.

Linda's routine of healthy eating and exercise was mandatory. Little did I know that it was saving my life, saving me from an actual emotional, psychological breakdown. My main function was to get up, get dressed, and get out. If I could only get up, get dressed and get out, I could make it to the next day. Another convenience of being at Linda's house was that it was just a few blocks from the middle school that Tamara was bussed to from our East Side Tacoma home.

Tamara attended this particular school and was bussed there because it was a school for highly capable learners, of which Tamara was one. Linda had extended her home to my entire family, but Joseph had chosen to stay somewhere else. Occasionally, he would come and spend the night. Linda was so wonderful that I could talk when I needed to talk. I could cry when I felt like crying. But she was careful not to let me wallow too long. She always redirected my energy into taking care of me. By taking care of me, Tamara was under my umbrella. She had me focus on staying healthy, because exercise was going to help with my major depression.

By March 16th, it was 30 days into the investigation and Joseph and I were still not really communicating a lot, due to what had happened the night of the murder and the infidelity issues. It was a subject matter that we tiptoed around. One early evening he had taken me to Linda's house. We sat in the car, and we discussed the night of the murder. He explained to me that he was with his friend and he didn't know why he led me to believe that they were gone. He told me that they had meant to leave, and decided at some point not to go.

I asked Joseph, "Why did you call me that morning and allow me to think that you were out of town; how you could say that you arrived in California; why couldn't you have just said that you were just leaving, or you were still on the road, or you had decided not to go? What was the big deal?"

His answers didn't make sense to me. It just wasn't enough. It wasn't until a few months later I had found out this information by way of his youngest sister; Joseph was with a woman named Brenda. Everyone in his family knew that he was still in town except for me.

Our voices began to get loud. The anger had finally oozed out and broke through like a boil filled with pus, a festering boil, you know it just grows until it comes to a point and busts, and all of the pus and infection starts to come out. I began to tell him how horrible I felt being interrogated by a white police officer that told me that my husband was a liar, and asked me what kind of wife, what kind of woman, would stay married to a man that would lie and cheat on her. I began to scream at him and tell him how degrading and dirty I felt as those white police officers kept asking me if I was having affairs with someone; that you Joseph said that I had been having an affair. I was angry that Joseph would leave our home unprotected, while he chose to be out partying with his friends.

Why would partying with his friends be more important than being at home with Tamara and me? Was our life, our marriage, so horrible for him that he had to plan stories of being out of town just to get away from me, just to get away from home? In October 1999 we reconciled from a three year separation. Joseph returned from his third Korean tour of duty and came back to me. In 2001, he had returned to the streets, returned to his usual episodes of disappearing, staying out, and excluding me. It's now February 2002 and I can't help but wonder why I was back here. What was my lesson to learn?

It was so unusual for him to go to such extremes because he had partied with his friends before, all night long, sometimes not returning home till the next morning. What was so different this time, that he would have to tell me that he was in another town, in another state.

The pain was much more than we both could imagine. He, too had been interrogated and called a liar, called a cheat. The police accused him of sleeping with his niece. He had to share this information with the military personnel as well. His 17-year military service in the United States Army was on the line. I had no answers. I didn't feel any better. I still felt that something was missing. It was just too extreme. I got out of the car and went into the house, took a shower, and cried myself to sleep.

The investigation was still going on. My house was just about finished with the repairs and the renovations from the murder, and it was time to return home. I left most of the renovation oversight to Joseph. I watched him oversee the renovation of our home, and wondered if he could oversee the renovation of our lives as well. I left all the communicating with the press to Joseph. He was the spokesperson for the Joseph Nichols family. I just had no words to say. God just literally closed my vocal cords.

Wandering Wilderness

By March 26th, it had been a little over 40 days and the house was almost finished. It was time to go back to our home. The neighbors from the community had left flowers and cards of condolences. People had lit candles and placed them on our porch. There were bouquets and plants everywhere. I remember turning on the TV at Linda's house and seeing news clips of our home and a neighbor walking up the path way with a gift and placing it on the porch and then leaving. The neighborhood was fairly quiet most of the time. I lived right on the bus line and our neighborhood was ethnically diverse. We lived within the Puyallup Native American Reservation in Tacoma, Washington. The neighbor's response to the tragedy was very consoling. They too, had been praying for our household. A neighbor named Heidi, whom I had never met before, left a book of prayers. Most of the neighbors had been interviewed by the detectives. The detectives were in the area daily looking for clues and any information that could be helpful.

One of my neighbors gave a police report of hearing a driver speed off in the alley around 7 o'clock or so. He said that because he was about to watch Billy Graham and the detectives checked and Billy Graham was airing around 7 p.m. The investigators also talked with Pierce County Transit to see what time the buses came during that same time frame. One of the bus drivers they contacted reported that there was a car blocking the pathway for the route of the bus driver, which caused him to have to awkwardly make his right turn. He reported that to his dispatch and the dispatcher shared that information with the detectives.

Another neighbor shared with detectives that she had seen two people parked in a car outside of the home for hours. She thought it was strange that the car had moved, left, then came back an hour or so later. All this talk and speculation continued to feed the local media. There was still so much speculation that the Nichols family members began to become angry with me. As we moved back into my home, the talk in the media was suggesting that this could have been my fault. I still decided to remain silent and allow Joseph to speak for me to the press.

I continued to check my voice messages. Prior to moving back home, I would go to the house and remove 50 messages at a time, people calling from everywhere, giving their condolences. There were so many calls that I would just write them down, write the names down, the date that they called, the phone number, and just tally a list until the day we moved back into my home. My answering machine was filled again. The maximum capacity was 50 calls.

One of my plans was to take advantage of family counseling. My pastor had offered to do family counseling. He had offered to consult with the entire Nichols family, to help us start the process of healing. I didn't know if the Nichols family would accept the offer. However, I still shared with them the invitation that my Pastor had extended. Well, it just so happened that they agreed, and we started family counseling with Joseph, his mother, and Keenya's mother. Tamara was there and I was there, too. The pastor opened the counseling session with a prayer. We had about three counseling sessions with our pastor. I was so thankful at how he was bridging some of the gap between me and other family members, a gap that had widened between me and other family members. We talked about how the investigation was going. We talked about how we could come together to get advocacy for Keenya. I was there to answer any questions that they may have had of me. But we all still just had no idea of who could have done this.

By May 16th, it had been about three months and our counseling continued. About six months had past and by August 16th, talks of us in the media had subsided a bit. I decided to go into deeper treatment, because Tamara and I needed more support. My daughter could no longer be left alone. She would no longer walk into the house by herself. She had nightmares at night, with dreams of her being shot in the face. Every night she would come into my bed and sleep with me.

And I, myself, could not sleep. If I went to sleep, I didn't stay asleep. I had reoccurring nightmares and pictures in my mind of Keenya's face and the bullet casing beside her head. I had dreams of Keenya lying at the mortuary. I had dreams of Keenya at the funeral. I had dreams of Keenya talking to me from her grave. I had anxiety everyday. I experienced thoughts of suicide.

My child dealt with so much pain, not just hers, but everyone else's. She just did not have the emotional skills to hide them. She had overheard Nichols family members say that it was my fault. That if I wasn't in other people's business, Keenya would be alive. She heard so much conversation from the Nichols family, that she didn't know how to protect me. I knew then that we were in trouble.

I began the search for more defined counseling. I shared with Tamara's father that we were going to get therapy and see if he wanted to come, but he refused. He said that he didn't need any therapy. Joseph also said that his daughter Tamara didn't need any therapy. I begged to differ and I told him, even if she didn't need therapy, we were going to get some before she needs it. That if we weren't crazy, we were going to get therapy so that we wouldn't go crazy. So, I set out to find an African-American, preferably female, therapist to do our counseling and therapy. I prayed that God would reveal a resource, because every African-American professional did not counsel adolescents, and Tamara was only 14.

One day I talked with my Delta Sigma Theta sorority sister Billie Johnstone, who was also a mental health professional and had her own practice. Billie had recently retired and little did I know that she was the only African-American female practitioner in the Tacoma area that provided mental health therapy for adolescents. I shared with Counselor Billie the nature of what was happening to us, and she agreed to come out of retirement and to counsel Tamara for me. Tamara and I both went to the sessions and we completed the questionnaire and intake information.

We were both diagnosed with post-traumatic stress disorder (PTSD), major depression and anxiety. I had not heard of post-traumatic stress disorder outside of it being something that military personnel would suffer, following combat engagement. So, the term was new to me, as it relates to my diagnosis with it. As I began to look at the research on post-traumatic stress disorder, I concluded that Tamara and I had every symptom. We fit the bill for this diagnosis. So our treatment began. Tamara was very reluctant and angry that I was insisting that she go to counseling. She had heard different comments, such as her father's, and had adopted the attitude about mental health therapy being negative, meaning that she was crazy. Actually, come to think of it, in the black community, any types of mental health issues are perceived as "going crazy."

I had to tell Tamara that I didn't care whether she sat there with her arms folded or not; we were going to go to therapy so that we would have it in place for us as we go through this. I explained to Tamara that she and I shared something that nobody else shared, that we saw Keenya in the devastation of the crime scene. Nobody else saw that. By the time everybody else saw Keenya she was dressed, looking like a princess asleep in the casket. We were the only ones to see what really happened. This was one of the main reasons why we were going to get help. I told Tamara that some people go to counseling because they are "crazy," but we were going to counseling so that we would not "go crazy." There would be help there to catch us, so we could deal with what was left of our lives. I told her that she could go by herself or we could go together, just as long as she goes.

During the first counseling session, Tamara did not participate very much. She did exactly as I thought, sat there with her arms folded. However, Counselor Billie was well equipped to get dialogue and start our counseling journey. Tamara decided that she wanted to go by herself because she thought she might want to share some things that she didn't want me to know. I said fine. Then we had made arrangements for Tamara to go after she got out of school, twice a week. By September 16th, a month had gone by, and Tamara decided she wanted me to go with her. I agreed. And so, we started going together. Counselor Billie prescribed medication for my anxiety and she sent me to a prescriptive therapist, who had prescriptive authority and confirmed Billie's diagnosis.

We didn't put Tamara on any type of medication at that time. We felt we could control it with diet and counseling. Tamara became more volatile. She also was very irritated most of the time. It was very hard for me to see my normal 14-year-old baby girl in this type of pain. She didn't know how to deal with her feelings and neither did I. I felt terrible every day, so I could imagine how she was feeling. I loved my child and I put all my personal strength in making sure she was going to be okay. My personal strength was all I had. I had none of my immediate family here, except for my stroke stricken, elderly father. There was just only so much that I was going to share with him. My father is a praying man. In my childhood, he was called the "praying deacon." That is where I needed him the most, on the threshing floor in prayer.

Emotional Cripple

It was October 2002 and eight months had gone by; there was nothing going on with Keenya's murder case. The investigation had no leads and therefore was placed in the cold case status of unsolved murders. The hype from the media was gone. Keenya's murder was no longer breaking news. The once shocked, curious, Tacoma community had returned to normal. There were a few calls coming to the house to check on our family. It was the preverbal today's news headlines had become tomorrow's trash can lining.

My life, as I had once known and lived, had changed drastically. Much of my feelings were raw. I was riddled with grief, remorse, and pain. Everyday I was in turmoil over Keenya's brutal murder. I was emotionally crippled to the point where I could not function. I had no drive or zeal for life anymore. I was spiraling down everyday. I tried to be normal. I tried to remember what normal was. The life of security, joy, and love was no longer my portion. I literally could not feel anything.

The one thing that I had to live for was my daughters, Tamara and Tasherra. Tamara's life was a wreck. My normal, witty, strong, and intelligent teenager was now a scared, insecure, angry, and traumatized fourteen year old. I was a traumatized, 42-year-old woman feeling as bad as I felt. Tamara was feeling what I was feeling, but without any skills to deal with the emotionally scarred feelings we both had. We couldn't communicate well at all. I knew I had to keep us in counseling. Tamara and I were hemorrhaging inside.

Tamara was a freshman in high school. The transition into high school for normal teenagers is challenging enough. Now she had to transition with this major tragedy in her life.

Tasherra, our oldest daughter, was 19 and away attending St. Augustine's College in Raleigh, North Carolina when Keenya was murdered. Tasherra was very close with her cousin before leaving for college. They loved each other. I could depend on Keenya to check in with my girls to make sure that they had someone to confide in. I don't know when Tasherra received the news about the tragedy that occurred in our home. Tasherra was independent and was strong in her faith in God. She was a praying child and now a praying young adult. I remember asking her to pray for me and to pray for her family. I could depend on her to go to the Lord. I thanked God that she was away. She was away from the rumors, the anger, resentment, and the animosity towards me that was building up in the Nichols family.

The Nichols family had begun to shut me out of their lives. I don't know if it was intentionally. They just did not want me around. My presence annoyed them, especially Keenya's mother. Joseph was the oldest son and most of his time was spent consoling his family. He was dealing with a lot of his own personal grief. Keenya was his oldest sister's daughter. The fact that she was killed in his home practically paralyzed him. He felt that he didn't protect her. She was in our home for protection and now she was dead. His loyalty to family was important to him. He has always felt responsible for his family; as a result, all except one sibling moved from California to Washington.

The divide between Joseph and I grew wider. He was mad with me all the time. He was irritable and cold. He was gone most of the time. He would be with his family. They all were mad at me. They were going places where I was not invited. Most of the time he did not tell me that he was leaving to go somewhere. He would just leave. I would receive a call from him on his cell calling to check in with our daughter Tamara. There were many times I needed to be held, but when I approached him I didn't feel it was a good idea. I don't remember him consoling me like he consoled so many other family members. He had nothing for me. So I went through my remorse and grief by myself.

Part Three – Revelation
D.C. Sniper Shootings Linked To Tacoma

Many evenings I would come home and turn on the television. It was just on out of habit. I didn't watch it much. While watching the news one evening, there was a story of people being shot and killed somewhere on the East Coast. I glimpsed at the broadcast for a moment. I wouldn't stay tuned too long, because my life was reeking with drama and trauma. The news broadcast came on again the next day; three more people were shot and killed. The broadcast said that these were sniper shootings. Someone was randomly shooting people in Virginia, Maryland, and now, Washington D.C. This was really terrorizing, because we were still dealing with the aftermath of the 9-11 terrorist attacks on the East Coast. Now there was a sniper shooting innocent people in D.C.

Everyday for a week there were more killings. Two women were killed in Alabama. People were being killed while pumping gas in Virginia and Maryland, and while leaving a grocery store. A child was shot near his school. A woman was killed while sitting at the bus stop. Another woman was killed loading supplies in her vehicle while leaving a Home Depot. A man was shot in the parking lot in front of his restaurant. He survived the bullets wounds in his chest. A taxi cab driver was killed. A city bus driver was killed while parked. The eastern part of our nation was under siege. It was apparent that we were being attacked domestically by terrorist cells residing in our country.

The news was full of experts and psychics giving profiles of who this killer was. They had profiled him as being a white male. There were interviews with serial killers trying to give some indication of the mindset of this mass murderer. Some said he was a militia rebel of some sort. Nothing could describe the vulnerability that our country was going through. The East Coast was paralyzed. The rest of the country was traumatized as we watched the latest developments.

It was Monday, October 24, 2002 when the latest development turned unusual. The trail for D.C. sniper investigation was leading to the State of Washington. There were helicopters and road blocks in a Tacoma neighborhood. The FBI and other agencies were now in Tacoma, Washington at the home of Robert Holmes. They were in his back yard sawing down a tree trunk looking for bullet casing that could match the bullets that were pulled out of the bodies of some of the victims.

How in the heck could this be connected to Robert Holmes? No one knew. Robert Holmes lived in Tacoma. I knew who he was because he served on the board of directors for the Al Davies Boys and Girls Club. He was the boxing coach at the club. He was respected in our community. He was John and Mildred Muhammad's good friend. Robert and John worked on car repairs together.

Now that the investigation was in Tacoma, I watched television relentlessly to find out how Robert Holmes was connected to the DC sniper murders. The speculation around town was buzzing, as our community waited anxiously to be apprised of the connection. The tree trunk and other fragments found in Holmes' backyard were taken to ballistics. Everything matched the bullets from the gun that was being used in Washington, D.C. The report was that the bullets matched came from a high powered Bushmaster Semi-automatic Rifle. Something similar to the military's M-16 Rifle. The latest murder was that of bus driver Conrad Johnson.

How did the D.C. murder investigators get a tip to link them to Robert Holmes in Tacoma, Washington? That was everyone's question. Robert Holmes notified the FBI that he knew who the sniper was. He called the task force and left the information. It took a few days for them to contact him back. Robert Holmes knew it was John when the media released the type of weapon that was used in the shooting on television. He had seen John with the Bushmaster at his home. John had built a special scope to the rifle. He showed it to Holmes.

He recalled that John found out where Mildred was living from a private investigator that was hired for him by the Devoted Dads Organization of Tacoma. That was the organization that John used to try to get legal rights to get his children back. When they told John that Mildred was in the D.C. area, they never heard from him again. Holmes said John came to his house and told him he knew where Mildred and the children were. The last time he spoke with John, he asked if he was going to do harm to Mildred. It was when Holmes saw the description of the rifle that he called the D.C. sniper task force. The investigation then moved from Tacoma to Bellingham, Washington. Bellingham is located near the border of Vancouver, Canada. What a stretch. Why Bellingham?

October 26, 2002 was the day that some complicated questions were answered. It was Wednesday and I had arrived home around 8:30 p.m. from Bible study. When I came in I turned on the television. The first thing I saw was John Allen Muhammad's face on the screen. Under his picture was the caption saying D.C. sniper suspect John Allen Muhammad. At the same time, the telephone rang and it was my husband Joseph. He sounded frantic, he asked where we had been and where was Tamara. I reminded him it was Wednesday night Bible study. I asked what was wrong? What was happening? He told me to turn on the television. I said I saw John Muhammad's picture on. He said that he was on his way home and to lock the doors. I sat down and listened to the news broadcast.

*John Lee Malvo, left,
and John Allen Williams*

AP Photo

John was a suspect in the D.C. sniper murders. There was also a young boy suspect named Lee Boyd Malvo. Looking at John's picture on the television was the eeriest feeling I ever had. John looked crazy and deranged. I actually knew the suspected mass murderer that had been terrorizing the nation to the point of canceling professional sporting events and placing whole communities on curfew. I knew the suspected mass murderer that killed 12 innocent people and shot a young child.

This was incomprehensible to me. My spirit inside of me was in turmoil. I had this spirit of heaviness weighing me down the whole day. I went to Bible study one hour early to pray, because I had felt spiritually heavy. It was a troubling spirit. I went to pray corporately, as well as privately for God to make known what the troubling spirit was for. I needed a revelation.

Joseph arrived home. We sat together and watched the latest developments. There was a search for John and the boy, Lee Boyd Malvo. The FBI had given a telephone number over the television for people to call with any information that could assist them in capturing John. I asked Joseph if we should call them. He said that his mother had called the number. He said he wanted to wait until I got home. I agreed we should call. When we called, an FBI agent answered. I told them that I knew John Muhammad and that we may have some information about him. They took my name and telephone number. The agent said someone would be calling me to take my information. She also said that they were receiving a lot of phone calls and it would take some time.

I could imagine the many incoming phone calls; John was well known in Tacoma as the mechanic of Express Car/Truck Mechanic Service. He worked on everyone's car at some point. He had been to many Tacoma homes doing tune-ups, oil changes, and minor repairs. Now his face is on national television as the suspect in the sniper murders.

The more we looked at John's picture, the more we thought about Mildred Muhammad and the children. They lived in Maryland with her sister.

The shootings were all around her. Some of the shootings were in the city where she lived. Joseph and I discussed the possibility of John being on the East Coast looking for Mildred and their children. What other reason would he have for going there?

I wondered what she was doing, looking at John's picture on the news. I wondered if she was safe. He had not been caught yet. Was she is danger? Was he looking for her and the children? I tried calling her cell phone, but it wasn't on. I got on the Internet to e-mail her. I asked her to call me and let me know if she and the children were okay. After all they had been through, now this. John is a suspected mass murderer!

I asked her who the boy was with John. I knew it was not his son, which was the speculation from the media. John has three children by Mildred. He had two other sons from previous marriages; both of whom I had met. I did not get any response from the e-mail I sent Mildred. She did not call me, which I thought was strange. This was something she would have called me about. I felt something was wrong. Something had to be going on for her not to call me.

In the next couple of days we were finally contacted by the FBI. Agent Marty Shane came over to the house. Amazingly, it was the same FBI Agent that Mildred spoke with to report her children missing almost two years ago. They told Mildred that they could not help her, because there was no proof that John had left the country with them. I gave him a good hard stare.

He was now in my house. He remembered me, and was familiar with Mildred and my relationship with John and Mildred. I just wanted to report to the FBI what had transpired with John taking the children and them being found in Bellingham, Washington. I told him that when the children were found, they were extradited to Tacoma and returned to Mildred. I shared with him how the court had awarded her custody and granted her permission to leave the state with them. John was devastated and angry.

I asked Agent Shane if he had heard from Mildred. He told me she and her children were in protective custody in Maryland. That explained why she didn't reply to my e-mails.

Joseph and I shared with Agent Shane that we felt that John could have tried to kill Keenya as retaliation for my helping Mildred when her children were found and released to her custody. Agent Shane confirmed that John and Lee were in Tacoma the day Keenya was murdered. They had been arrested a couple of days before at Market Place Grocery Store on Pearl Street for shoplifting. They were let go. There was just too much coincidence going on. Mildred's children were found in Bellingham, Washington. The D.C. sniper investigation went from Tacoma to Bellingham. There was connection to me. More connection to me than I could ever imagine.

The next breaking news we received was the capture of John Allen Muhammad and Lee Boyd Malvo while sleeping in a rest area in Maryland. They were spotted by a truck driver who recognized the car and the description of the two and called state patrol. The two were surrounded, arrested, and taken into custody. They were in a late model Chevy Caprice, to the contrary of a white van description given earlier. The car they were in had a hole carved in the trunk. The back seat was removable, so they could lay down and shoot through the hole. The car had a laptop computer inside of it. Then the news showed the police removing a small tripod and a rifle from the car.

I was on my couch, balled up in a fetal position, watching this live nightmare on my television. I couldn't move. I felt something inside of me being ripped apart. I knew that this was connected to me is some horrid way. My life was in the darkest season. I was in the eye of a horrible storm.

The next day, I received a phone call from the Tacoma Police Department stating that a man came to them with his weapons. He told the police that after seeing John Muhammad's picture on the news he needed to turn in his weapons. John and Lee had stayed with him for three weeks in February and had access to his weapons. The police stated that they sent the weapons to ballistics. The gun was a .45 caliber semi-automatic handgun. There was a match to his gun that matched the bullet found in Keenya. I asked if they were going to arrest the gun owner. The police said they had no reason to suspect him. They felt he was being honest, sincere, and wanted to help if possible. They had no reason or indication to think he was Keenya's killer. The police would not give me his name. They said that he had to remain anonymous because the investigation was on-going.

There was the horrible connection. I was devastated. Keenya was possibly murdered by John Muhammad. The police said they had not tied the weapon to John; however they were going to look for DNA. The DNA testing would take a few weeks. Keenya's mother and the rest of the Nichols' family were given the same information. Everyone was sure that he had done this to our Keenya. Why? John Muhammad's connection to Keenya's murder was obscure to say the least. The motive was not clear at the time. However, my spirit was troubled. My mind was running a video of events that had occurred with Mildred and the return of her three children that John had abducted from their school. I was in the courtroom with Mildred the day that her children were released into her custody.

Lee Boyd Malvo

AP Photos

Trauma of My Drama II

The media was in sniper story frenzy. Now my house was on television again, not just locally but nationally. This time it was tied to John Allen Muhammad, Lee Boyd Malvo, and Keenya's murder. We received a call from Detective Webb from the Tacoma Police Department. He said he wanted the entire family to meet at the station. They had finished their investigation and wanted to discuss it with the family before holding a formal press conference.

My oldest sister, Sheila, was in Tacoma visiting with me during the time all this was going on. Only God knew that I would need her on this particular day. I had been going through Keenya's tragedy alone. My family wanted me to come home. They wanted to support me and wanted me back in San Diego. I was their baby sister, and they were willing to do whatever I needed to get me out of Washington. They pleaded on many occasions for me to just come home. They knew that Joseph was not being there for me. They knew that his family had turned their backs on me. They knew that way before I realized it. Why did I stay? They pleaded and asked me many times to come to San Diego. I rationalized in my mind that my children needed stability. The real reason was that I did not want to return home without anything. I did not feel that I was successful or had accomplished anything significant. I did not want to return home. I specialized in focusing on others, that way I would not have to deal with my feelings.

My sister and I arrived at the police station, and went to the conference room to join the rest of the Nichols' family. When we arrived, seated at the table was Joseph, my daughter Tamara, and the entire Nichols family. We spoke and took a seat at the table. We were waiting for the Detective to come in when Keenya's boyfriend, entered. I had not seen him since he was released from jail. I heard he was coming by often to see his baby girl. Everyone greeted him; Joseph stood and gave him a hug. As I stared at the warm embrace that he had received from Joseph, all I could do was wonder why Joseph had not embraced me? All I could think in my head was how my husband could embrace the man that physically abused his niece. I didn't know this man at all, other than he was Angeleah's dad. All I could think of was how easy it appeared for him to embrace this man, and I never received one embrace from Joseph through this whole ordeal. I tried really hard to remember.

I began feeling really strange. I looked at each one in that room differently that day. It all became clear to me after the affectionate embrace of Keenya's boyfriend. They really did not care about me. They blamed me for Keenya's murder. Blood was thicker than water, and I was not their blood.

Detective Webb entered the conference room, along with the police department's public relations person. He thanked everyone for coming. He said that the department was going to hold a press conference to inform the public that the bullet found in Keenya matched a gun that a man had turned into the police. He would not say the name of the man the gun belonged to, only that he was cooperative and they didn't feel he had anything to do with Keenya's murder. John and Lee had stayed with this person for three weeks. John had access to this man's weapons. When John's picture appeared on the television, this mystery man brought all his weapons to the police department.

John Muhammad was now officially a suspect in the murder of Keenya Cook. John was in Tacoma the day that Keenya was shot. The police believed that John's intended target was me, Isa Nichols. They believed John held a vendetta against me for helping his wife regain custody of their children. The detective asked if anyone had any questions. They would answer any questions as long as it would not harm their ongoing investigation.

My sister slowly grabbed my hand. She squeezed my hand so hard that I looked at her. She wanted to get my attention. When I looked, she was rolling a $10 dollar bill in her hand. She then whispered that she was giving me energy. She was going to put the money in my hand; when I received it I was to give it back to her. She said to concentrate on the energy. I did what she said. I was so focused on the energy, that I didn't hear the questions that were being asked. I just focused on the energy. I could hear voices, but I wasn't focused on whose voice it was. I could hear comments that said, "All I care about is Keenya." "All I care about is what happened to Keenya." "The only thing that matters is Keenya."

I looked up at my daughter Tamara. She looked so confused. She just stared at everyone talking around the table. I wanted to reach across the table and cover her. Cover her ears. She actually heard that these two criminals came to her home to kill her mother, and now all that mattered was Keenya. I did not matter! She did not matter! I just wanted to cover her impressionable mind. I knew that my little girl would never be the same.

The detectives apologized to the family, and told us that they would be in contact with us. They wanted to ask me some questions and they would contact me. Everyone stood up and left the conference room. I sat for a moment processing that John had come to kill me. The bullet that killed Keenya was meant for me. We were slowly walking in the parking lot to our vehicles when I began to stand still. My feet felt like lead in my shoes. I could not take another step.

My sister turned and noticed that I was standing in the middle of the parking lot. Sheila came back and stood in front of me. She grabbed my arms and began to squeeze me real tight. She squeezed me so hard that I could feel her hand touching my bone. Tears began to swell up in my eyes. Sheila told me not to cry.

"You better not cry, not now, not in front of the Nichols!" She said that they were not my family. I have my own family; a family that loves me. I was her family.

"Don't you realize I am your family," she said. "You better not shed one tear in front of them!"

She held my hand and we walked back to the car. When we got in the car I didn't know where to go, so we just drove around. My sister was so angry. She was cursing and saying how dare them. How dare they say those things about me. How could they say it was only about Keenya? I was Joseph's wife, Tasherra and Tamara's mother! They preferred you dead. How could they say the things they said in front of my daughter, Tamara?

We were the breaking news story, but this time all over the world. We were on every network, and in every newspaper. When I arrived home, the media was camped outside our door for blocks. My sister and I looked at the reporters. I didn't want to talk to them. We just drove by them. We couldn't go home. I decided to go back over to my good friend Linda Braddy's house, where I stayed and took refuge for a couple of months when the murdered happened. Here I was at her doorstep again; this time with my sister. I prayed that Linda would be home. I couldn't think of anywhere else we could go.

Linda opened the door with her usual warm smile. She was chipper and warm spirited. She invited us inside. She took one look at us and asked us what was going on. I asked her if she had watched television. She said she had saw pictures of my house on there, but she thought it was the same story stuff. I shared with her the latest developments.

My sister interrupted me and told Linda that I was in real trouble. She began to explain to Linda the details of the meeting at the police department. Linda listened attentively as she made us some tea. She made us so comfortable. She insisted that we stay at her home for the night. We took her up on the hospitality. My sister had spoken with Linda over the phone many times in the past while I was staying with her. She was grateful that I had Linda for a friend, a friend indeed, because we couldn't go back to my house for awhile.

I was exhausted. I didn't have much to say. I was still devastated. My emotions were raw. I didn't feel safe. I felt so vulnerable. I just didn't know what to do with all the information. Where would I go from this point on? I felt so empty inside. The only thing I could do was pray. I wanted to pray, but I could not get any words out. I just knew that God would hear the matters in my heart. My heart was shattered and it physically hurt. I needed Him. I needed to know that He was with me. I was surely walking through the shadows of death, and evil was present around me. I needed God to comfort me. The enemies were at my table. I needed His mercy, and I needed it now! I woke up the next morning to find this in the New York Times headlines:

Retracing A Trail: An Earlier Killing; With Maryland Arrest, Tacoma Family Finds An Answer

By NICK MADIGAN
Published: October 30, 2002

To the Nichols family, John Muhammad was just a guy who came by with his three kids for barbecues in the backyard, an adept auto mechanic with an eye for detail and an air of conviction.

Some members of the family had known him as long as 10 years— though never closely, even after Mr. Muhammad hired Isa Nichols, an accountant, to keep his books at his auto repair business on East Portland Avenue.

"Last time I saw him," over a year ago, "was at a barbecue," Pamala Nichols, Isa's 45-year-old sister-in-law, said today. "We were very cordial."

Things began to go wrong, the family says now, when Isa Nichols took sides with Mr. Muhammad's former wife Mildred in a custody dispute over the couple's three children. Even so, the family never suspected him when Keenya Cook, 21, Pamala Nichols's daughter, answered the door on Feb. 16 and was shot to death.

Then, after Mr. Muhammad and Lee Malvo were arrested in Maryland last Thursday in the sniper shootings around Washington, D.C., it all suddenly began to make sense.

When Mr. Muhammad's face appeared on television in connection with that arrest, shocked members of the Nichols family called the police and the F.B.I., saying he might have been the person who killed Ms. Cook with a shot to the head while her 6-month-old baby lay in bed upstairs.

On Monday, after the authorities had also been alerted by a friend with whom Mr. Muhammad shared an interest in firearms, the Tacoma police identified Mr. Muhammad and Mr. Malvo as chief suspects in the Cook killing and in a shooting in early May at a synagogue here in which no one was hurt. The police linked the pair to the Tacoma shootings after performing ballistics tests on two handguns that they were found to have borrowed from Mr. Muhammad's friend, who is said to have lent the authorities much cooperation and has not been identified.

Mr. Muhammad "started here, by killing my daughter," Pamala Nichols said today. "He killed my child first."

"He's a coldblooded killer," said Isa Nichols's husband, Joseph, an Army staff sergeant, standing in the very doorway where his niece, who lived with him and his wife, was shot.

Ms. Cook, he said, was the one member of the household who had never met Mr. Muhammad.

"He didn't know her," Sergeant Nichols said. "I think he just wanted to bring torment to the family. He didn't care who was at the door."

Sergeant Nichols had never found anything particularly odd about Mr. Muhammad, although he was evidently strict with his children. "Whenever he was around, they'd sit and not talk too much, but when he wasn't around, they'd play like normal kids," Sergeant Nichols said, echoing frequent descriptions of Mr. Muhammad's overbearing demeanor toward Mr. Malvo.

Still, "I would never have associated him with being a deranged killer," Sergeant Nichols said.

Sergeant Nichols said his wife and Mildred Muhammad had become good friends. When Mr. Muhammad disappeared for a time with the couple's children during their custody battle, Isa Nichols, who also kept the books for a battered-women's shelter, appeared in court on behalf of Mrs. Muhammad and "helped her find the right people to talk to so that she could get her kids back," Sergeant Nichols said.

Until then, Mr. Muhammad had been someone on whom the family occasionally called to repair vehicles. "He was a genius with cars," Pamala Nichols said.

Mr. Muhammad's skill perhaps proved useful later: the police who seized the 1990 Chevrolet Caprice in which he and Mr. Malvo were found sleeping last week said its rear seat and trunk had been modified into a sniper's perch.

Pamala Nichols, who lives with her own mother, Jean Nichols, in southwest Tacoma, said she had resented her sister-in-law, Isa, in the aftermath of Ms. Cook's death.

"My child was killed wrongfully," said Ms. Nichols, who has two other children, in their 20's. "It was meant for Isa. If it wasn't for her, my daughter wouldn't be dead."

As she spoke, her granddaughter, Ms. Cook's child, Angeleah Ashani Yvés Rogers, now 14 months old, played at her feet. "This baby was her best friend," Ms. Nichols said. "They'd stay up till 2 or 3 in the morning, playing."

The toddler's father, Angelo Rogers, a rapper who goes by the name Slayer tha Player, was questioned by the police after Ms. Cook's killing.

"He's a cool guy, and I want people to leave him alone," said Jean Nichols, Ms. Cook's grandmother, the family matriarch. "He was depressed and being seriously maligned by people, but the family has exonerated him."

Jean Nichols described the death of her granddaughter as "a horrible, terrible ordeal — worse than when my father died, worse than when my husband died."

After the arrests in Maryland last week, she recalled, "my son called me and said, 'Look at the TV — it's John, Mom.' As soon as I saw his face on TV, I called the F.B.I."

She said her granddaughter had been "an outgoing, wonderful girl who hung out with her family."

Ms. Cook, born on March 11, 1980, in Fairfield, Calif., lived for a few years in Woodbury, N.J., with her paternal grandfather, before reuniting with her mother in Tacoma when she was 15. Shortly after that, she auditioned in Seattle for a modeling job with 1,200 others, two of them her first cousins Tasherra and Tamara. All three were among the half-dozen finalists, but none got the job. "That really upset her," her mother remembered. "She cried all the way home from Seattle. She kept saying, 'I'm the prettiest; I'm the best-looking one, Mom.' "

John Came To Kill Me

The next morning, my sister and I went back to my house. We were able to get in without being stopped. We were inside about twenty minutes when the door bell rang. I could see that it was some reporters. I just let the door bell ring and didn't answer it. We turned on the news to see the house. The media cameras had filmed my sister and me coming into the house. The media were filming the house with live coverage. The phone was ringing with reporters asking for an interview. Neighbors and friends were calling to see if there was anything I needed.

It had started all over again. I was more intense than on February 16, 2002, when Keenya was murdered. This time, my home was the D.C. snipers first murder scene. I was the Genesis to a trail that left thirteen people dead and a nation traumatized. John was in custody. He was found sleeping in a car at a rest stop in Maryland. I couldn't imagine what Mildred was feeling like. John was so close to where she lived. I tried calling Mildred but I could not get any answer. I didn't know what had happened to them. A few days had gone by and I heard nothing from Mildred. I needed to talk to her. My world was now out of sync. The reality that John had come to kill me was turmoil. I tried e-mailing her.

I wrote:

Fri, 25 Oct 2002 20:30:11 -0700 (PDT)

From:	"Isa Nichols" View Contact Details Add Mobile Alert
Subject:	please know!!!
To:	"Mildred Muhammad"

"please know that you are loved very, much. please don't let anything tell you any different. GOD has a plan for you and me, you are HIS child. please don't ask why, just know that no weapon formed against you will prosper and that you will be triumphant. please know that you have blessed many, many people. please know that you are a blessing, and you are from a royal priesthood. please know that you are fearfully and wonderfully made. please know that you were given gifts, their names are Lil John, Selena, Taalibah. please know that!

PLEASE KNOW THAT FEAR STEMS FROM NO LOVE; PERFECT LOVE CASTS OUT FEAR.....PLEASE KNOW THAT GOD LOVES YOU AND SO DO I.

I'm okay.....I'm strong, and so are you....we have to be Millie!!!!!

There was no reply to my e-mails. I wondered why Mildred had not called when she found out about John's being linked to Keenya's murder. I felt something was wrong; I wanted her to know what I was feeling. I did not blame her for John's decision to try to kill me. Mildred and I had been through so much in the past couple of years. We had no idea that this was going to be the outcome. We had done all we could do to advise the Tacoma authorities to get John at the onset of his demented and diabolical rampage. This was just incomprehensible.

When I did not hear from Mildred, things just ran rampant in my mind. Why wasn't she calling me? Didn't she care about what I was going through, knowing that John had tried to murder me and mistakenly killed Keenya instead?

I woke up one Saturday morning with Mildred and her children on my mind and in my heart. I decided to try the cell phone number I had one more time. It rang and Mildred answered the phone. Mildred screamed my name at the top of her lungs. She said that the FBI had taken her and the children into protective custody. They had to leave immediately. They even took her sister and family away from the home. She said they had her home under surveillance. They were already on to John, and figured out he was coming to get to her and the children. She could not make any phone calls. She didn't have access to any computer to check emails. It was so consoling to hear her voice. I felt a release of pressure now that I knew she was okay.

Mildred shared with me that she felt it could be John doing the random shooting. John's threats to destroy her would always be in her mind. He had picked up their children from school one day, took them to the airport, and boarded a plane for the island nation of Antigua, in the British West Indies. They were gone for eighteen months without a trace. He would call to say that she would never see them again. He promised that she would not live to raise their children. She always looked on roof tops and around the vicinity when she was out and about town. It was only a matter of time before John would show up. In fact, the shooting at the Michaels' store was one that Mildred often frequented. Many times she felt that the D.C. sniper shootings were in some way meant for her, and that John wanted her to know he was there.

Our conversation shifted to the media frenzy. The breaking news coverage of John and Lee Malvo's capture intrigued us both. There were so much speculation and inconsistency. One thing that was incorrect was that Lee Malvo was John's biological son. Mildred's children had shared with her that they played with Lee Malvo while in Antigua. I knew nothing about the whole Antigua story line. I knew that once Mildred and her children got settled, they would share what went on in their lives in Antigua.

I told Mildred that I was invited to be on television shows. Producers from networks were calling to fly me to the East Coast to appear on their shows. Connie Chung, Stone Phillips, and Larry King had left messages on my phone. Some of them had left business cards on my door. It was apparent that this story was huge. Our story was huge. John and Lee had terrorized the entire East Coast for several weeks.

What were we going to do? Mildred's response was to do whatever was necessary to make some money. I laughed, but she was serious. She had a point. Sheriff Moose was already offered a book deal. He didn't know the half of the things we knew. I envisioned us co-authoring our stories of love, family, and betrayal. The traumas from our dramas could give encouragement to many abused women in our communities.

Making money just didn't appeal to me. I had chosen to stay out of the media. After Keenya's death, I didn't trust the media. I had agreed to do an interview with our local CBS or NBC affiliate in Tacoma if it could benefit baby Angeleah. I wanted them to inform the community of the trust that was set up for Keenya's baby girl. They agreed. When the broadcast was aired, they said very little about the trust. I was furious. The media is powerful and persuasive. When there are stories involving white victims, they broadcast and avidly ask people to support. They could raise large sums of money, depending on what they put into it. They were not interested in this little baby girl that was left here. From then on, I just didn't care to talk to any of them. They were like vultures.

I watched television interviews with Keenya's family members. The media would capitalize on their rawest emotions. The hurt, anger, and resentment that Keenya took a bullet that was meant for me was what they captured. That hurt, anger, and resentment was targeted at me. The news media aired it as often as they could. They wanted to give me an opportunity to rebut, but I refused.

They wanted to know why Keenya was living with me. That was a whole other twenty-one-year old story. I didn't choose to put Keenya's mother through anymore than she needed to go through. I loved her enough to just leave it alone. I wasn't going to let the media put her, or myself, in an emotional battle. We both were in pain, we both were in trauma.

I did not realize the sacrifice I was making to keep the media out of our personal lives. My deciding not to say anything to the media, allowed for much speculation and erroneous communication. Everyone had a perspective as to why John had killed Keenya. The most shocking for me was when one article wrote that Keenya died because of me. The Chicago Times reporter had interviewed Keenya's mother and made it the headline with a full page picture of Keenya's mother. These people that I loved for over twenty years blamed me for the death of their family member to the Chicago Times.

Abandoned

Isolation and abandonment was on every hand. This ordeal was so huge. It was overwhelming. It became too much to share with the closest of family. It was real. It was scary. The only person that I could talk to was Mildred Muhammad. I could talk to her because it didn't require much. We had been through so much. We had shared so much. Mildred was putting a life together for herself and her children. She was just as isolated as I was. She was the ex-wife of a man who terrorized our nation's capital; John Muhammad, the notorious D.C. sniper.

It was March 2003 and Mildred had responded to an e-mail that I wrote to her. I had shared with her how bad I was feeling. I was feeling vulnerable, disappointed, and isolated. She responded back to me discerning how I needed badly to talk to someone.

She wrote: "Isa, I'm here. You don't have to explain to me that you need to talk. I know that honey! I am here for you as you are there for me. We have a special bond. That has been since I came to you for help with taxes. Some things we can't ignore, for now, I'm just trying to figure out through patience and prayer, where or how I can make money for personal items, little things the children need, to pay for school activities they want to be apart of, and small bills. It's difficult to try to live without money. But you know how I am. If you know my condition, why should I ask? Maybe that is the wrong way to think, but the people around me know and they don't appear as though they want to help. Kind of like it was when I was back there. So my attitude is that I made it there, I will make it here by the grace and mercy of God. Allah knows my heart and he will put people in place to help me. So I am leaning and depending on him and his promises. I have three examples to look at each day that his promises are true (John, Salena and Taalibah).

Have you heard anything from Dateline? You know you can contact me anytime day or night. You know that! Love Ya, Mildred."

I had heard from NBC's Dateline. Producers Stone Phillips and Debbie Goodison had wanted to do a story. Prior to them Geraldo Rivera, Larry King, and Connie Chung's producers had contacted me for an interview. I would often share with Mildred who the latest media contacts were, even though I had refused to be interviewed. I was in so much pain, I just wasn't prepared to have that level of media attention. I told Dateline's producers that I would give them an exclusive if they would wait to do their story. I told them that there was more to the D.C. snipers that the world is not aware of. There was a different story that no one knew existed. The true story of the D.C. snipers is a story of domestic abuse, domestic violence, and the lack of law enforcement. A story of betrayal.

When I shared this particular information with Mildred, she became irritated. I really had not understood her apprehension. I really didn't think she was serious, until she became delirious with tears. She claimed that I was betraying her trust. She had confided in me her most personal things between her, her husband, John, and I. Whatever I would be using to talk about or write about she did not want me to. She accused me of trying to profit from her tribulations. She even went so far as to tell me that she was going to contact her attorney to stop me.

My response to this sudden change from the woman who once encouraged me to profit anyway I could was confusion. I didn't even understand what she was accusing me of. I had not made any commitments to anyone. I assured Mildred that I had a story of my own. My own story was one that involved me and my family members. No matter what I said, Mildred's fear and anger escalated. She threatened to sue me. At first, I reacted with the same arrogance and intensity. I told her she could sue me.

I did not need her story; I had one of my own. I have a story about me, about Keenya. She didn't know Keenya Cook. Keenya Cook and Isa Nichols is a story in and of itself. That was a story of a young mother's courage and sacrifice; a story of domestic abuse and domestic violence. It was a story of the courage a young mother who had to get her and her baby out of harms way, only to meet her fate of being murdered by Mildred's husband, John. Why would she want to sue me for sharing my story?

I couldn't believe that after all we had survived, we had succumbed to this. My friendship and relationship for Mildred was real. I had been on the front line with her, even when she couldn't stand on her own. My friend had succumbed to fear me, that I would harm her in some way. I wrote to her on many occasions my thoughts, fears, and my deepest emotions. When her husband John, and boy accomplice Lee Malvo, were captured, it was evident that fate had catapulted us into areas we never could have imagined.

On September 16, 2003 I wrote what was on my mind and heart:

"Mildred, I Love You and Always Will. ...*When someone is in your life for a reason, it is usually to meet a need you have expressed outwardly. They have come to assist you through a difficulty, to provide you with guidance and support, to aid you physically, emotionally or spiritually. They may seem like a godsend and they are. They are there for the reason you need them to be. Then, without any wrong doing on your part or an inconvenient time, this person will say or do something to bring the relationship to an end. Sometimes they die. Sometimes they walk away. Sometimes they act up and act out and force you to take a stand.*

"What we must realize is that our need has been met, our desire fulfilled and our work is done. The prayer you sent up has been answered and it is now time to move on. When people come into your life for a season, it is because our turn has come to share, grow, or learn. They may bring you an experience of peace or make you laugh. They may teach you something you have never done. They usually give you an unbelievable amount of joy. Believe it! It is real! But...only for a season.

"Lifetime relationships teach you lifetime lesson; those things you must build upon in order to have a solid emotional foundation. Your job is to accept the lesson, love the person/ people anyway, and put what you have learned to use in all other relationships and areas of your life. It is said that love is blind, but friendship is clairvoyant.

"Thank you for being a part of my life. May GOD hold you in the palm of HIS hand and may HIS Angels watch over you."

"This excerpt is from something I read that touched me so profoundly. They are the words to the emotions that filled my heart after our last discussion. It was never my intention to do or say anything to betray our bond or our trust. I explained the best way I could that I was no threat to you. I wasn't going to revisit the subject again. I'm letting you know that I spoke with my attorney about me and my relationships. I found an attorney that I trusted. I have known him for awhile. I shared some things with my attorney, and I am going to continue. My attorney has the same code of ethics that your attorney does. Do you talk about me with your attorney? Do you share with him who I was, how our relationship began? Does he have a right to know? Do you trust him? If so, why? It was you and your attorney's advice for me to find an attorney of my own. I just didn't understand why you would think I would deliberately, knowingly betray you, other than fear that you would lose me as a friend. The only way that would happen is if you walked away, if you turned away.

"I have shared everything with you. Everything! I told you that I would not write anything or submit anything that you did not review. I have not gone back on that. My intentions are to do what I know to do spiritually and professionally, and that is to operate in truth ethically and lay the most proper and efficient foundation for myself. I will use what Satan meant to destroy me and with God in the midst, directing my path, use it to save others.

"You and I talked about me going out with my story first. I thought you meant that. You said you were not ready. I agreed, because you said you would support me and be there as a team with me, to look for and expose where the explosive mines are. I envisioned it just like back in the Phoebe House days. You trusted me then, why not now? Mildred, I still need your support and your friendship. I don't want to be in this alone, because without you, I'm alone in this thing. It has been very painful. My family living in San Diego, California is in shock and they are frightened for me. So I dare not share more than they could bear. I haven't even grieved for my niece Keenya yet.

"Millie, I supported you because you needed my support. I was there whenever you needed me. When we made the vow to one another, we had no idea what the cost or sacrifice would be for you and me. We made that vow of friendship with John listening right there in our midst. Now, you are out of physical danger and you have your children back in your life. They are healthy and they love their mom. GOD is going to supply all you need, according to HIS riches and glory, according to the power that works within you. You are exhausted and I am exhausted, but GOD will renew our strength. Our needs are different. Tamara is volatile and traumatized and blames me for helping you and everything else that is wrong in her life. She has said she hates me. I cry often because I don't want to lose the battle for her future. I'm sure you have your challenges too with teenagers, Lil' John and the girls, if not, you will.

"Mildred, you say you need money. Sheriff Moose could get money advanced to him for only doing his job, than so can we. We know the truth!

AP Photo

"They even have Sherriff Moose dolls! If someone wants to advance me some money to share a story of real truth that has no ending in sight; then whenever I should decide to share it, then yes, I'm taking it. I will send you a portion. If you don't want it, send it back. No hard feelings, no questions asked. I will not be insulted. I will put it in a trust for our children, for when they become adults. Please believe that I don't care about the money. I will not be made a fool of by not getting the knowledge and instruction to protect you and me. Using wisdom, as I have always done for many years professionally and in business, being slow to speak, eager to listen, and then discern. I could not say all of this until now, now that I have heard your pain. I heard your fear and concern. I do care and I always will."

Well to no avail, Mildred and I could not get through it. My appeal to give her assurance failed. Somehow we shut down. We shut down seven years of trust, communication, and most importantly, friendship. We could get through all the things that came our way, but now we went on silent mode. I didn't have a choice. She was the only someone that could feel the depths of what I felt. Without her, I was in this nightmare drama alone. Several months went by without my friend Mildred.

The Trial of John Muhammad and Lee Malvo

"The Trial of the Century" is what the media entitled it. John Allen Muhammad and Lee Boyd Malvo's trial began in the Commonwealth of Virginia. Although most of the murders were in the Maryland/Washington D.C. area, a decision had been reached to try them in Virginia. Virginia state law allowed for the death penalty for minors. Lee Malvo was a minor when he committed these murders, and was going to be tried as an adult. The ultimate punishment in the state was the death penalty. All the jurisdictions where these murders occurred agreed that Virginia would be the place to try John Mohammad for the murder of Dean Harold Meyers, and Lee Boyd Malvo for the murder of FBI Analyst Linda Franklin.

Both trials were held within weeks of each other. The investigation into all of the crime scenes was extensive, as well as expensive. The prosecuting attorneys had a lot of information. The public defense attorneys for John and Lee were the best in their field. They were attorneys with excellent and exceptional defense trial experience, with strategies that won verdicts of life in prison without parole. Where would they begin to put this horrid timeline of terror into perspective? They traveled in teams around the country to many of the crime scenes interviewing witness after witness. They interviewed victims that had survived their encounter with the deadly duo. The crime scenes and clues were collected from the states of Washington, Arizona, Alabama, and Louisiana, all the way to Washington, D.C. A timeline developed of many murder scenes that precipitated the D.C. murders.

Keenya Cook was now the focus of the prosecution team. The last murder scene connected to the D.C. sniper trail, was now recognized as the first murder scene. They had finally found the Genesis of this nation's domestic terrorists. I received a call from Detective Webb informing me that the prosecution team from Washington, D.C. was in Tacoma and wanted to speak with me and my daughter Tamara. I told the detective that I would meet with them first. I was asked to come down to the police station.

When I arrived to the police station, I went up to the floor where the detective offices were located. When I arrived, it was crowded. I didn't know who was who or what was what. I felt that this thing was huge. I felt confused. My stomach was in knots. Something was wrong with this picture. I felt I needed help.

I didn't let Detective Webb know that I had arrived. My spirit was deeply troubled. I realized I had to get up out of there. I left the office and went downstairs to call my friend and practicing attorney. Gerald Burke. I wanted to know more about what they would require from me. I could not get a signal on my cell phone, so I used the public phone. I called Attorney Gerald's office and asked to speak with him. I told his secretary that I was at the police station and it was imperative that I talk with him. God was working that day, because Gerald was in his office. I had called for him many times and seldom reached him on the first try. He was usually in court or in a meeting with a client. He answered in his usual professional demeanor, "This is Attorney Burke." I gasped and didn't hesitate to tell him where I was.

Attorney Burke's instructions were to get up and leave. He said that I should not be talking without an attorney, that this case was too huge. Gerald had been contacted by the press when John Muhammad was first arrested. The media had found out that he had counseled John in a custody case involving his son, Lynberg. There would not be anyway of me to know what their intentions were or what my information would be used for. He said to leave and call them back. He told me to tell them that I would not meet with them without an attorney and that I could not afford one. That was it for me, I left there. That was the feeling that prompted me to call Gerald in the first place. I felt that in my spirit when I arrived at the detective's office. God placed that feeling inside of me. Gerald was absolutely correct, because this was the onset of the trial of the century.

On September 15, 2003 the Circuit Court of Prince William County, Commonwealth of Virginia issued a summons, or subpoena, for me to appear as a material and necessary witness in the Virginia murder trial of Dean Harold Meyers. Dean Harold Meyers was murdered in Virginia while pumping gas at a gas station. My daughter Tamara, who was now 16-years-old, was issued one as well. We were notified that Prince William County Commonwealth's Attorney Paul Ebert wanted our testimony in the event John Muhammad was convicted; we were going to testify in the sentencing phase of the trial.

I received a telephone call from Prosecutor Richard Conway. He wanted to explain to me more about our testimony. We could not testify during the initial trial, because Keenya's murder, or any of the earlier murders, were not material to Dean Harold Meyers' case. Attorney Conway was compassionate, yet professional, in our conversation. He made me feel like my experience was worth hearing. He convinced me that it would be good to allow Tamara to tell her story. The mother whose son survived his shooting while at school, had the same concern for her son taking the witness stand. He shared that he testified and did well. It brought closure for him and his family. It would bring closure for Tamara. I was hesitant, but I said I would talk it over with Tamara's therapist. I wanted to make sure she could handle it emotionally. I asked Tamara if she wanted to participate. She agreed. This would be an opportunity for me to tell my story. This gave Keenya's death significant importance. She did not deserve to die. John Muhammad should be held accountable for her death. For the first time I felt that someone cared that Keenya was slain like an animal at my front door. Up until this time, the Tacoma authorities had not advocated for our case. They just were not going to spend their resources to pursue Keenya's killer. Their plan was to sit back and wait for the Virginia trials to conclude. She was the first murder victim that the rest of the world knew nothing about. There is no description that describes my relief for Keenya to be included in John's trial.

Attorney Conway explained that our testimony would only be used if they got a conviction against John. After the conviction, the trial would enter a sentencing phase. The sentencing phase would allow testimony about John and Lee's other crimes. The jury had two options to consider in the penalty phase of the trial, the death sentence or life in prison. Prosecutor Conrad wanted the jurors to see the maliciousness of their actions in the other shootings.

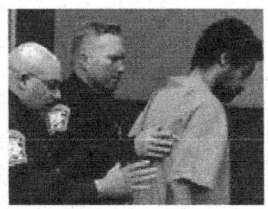

Convicted sniper John Allen Muhammad

AP Photo

Tamara and I boarded the plane for Virginia. The Commonwealth of Virginia paid for our airfare, meals, and hotel accommodations. We were taken to their task force headquarters. We were flown in on the very day the verdict was scheduled to be read. We were going to be there long enough for the jury to hear both our testimonies. If we wanted to see the trial, we could only do so after the judge released us as witnesses.

When we checked into the hotel, I couldn't help but notice the other witnesses from Tacoma. There were a host of us that had been subpoenaed from Tacoma. Most of them were police officers, forensic officers, and investigators that responded to Keenya's murder at my home. Robert Holmes, a close friend of John Muhammad, was on the list. There was one name that I did not recognize, a man that I had not seen before. He was quiet, reserved, but nervous at the same time. He looked weird. He was smoking cigarettes one after the other, always holding his head down toward the ground. His name was Earl Dancy, Jr. Who he was, and why he was there, would come out in the trial. He was one of the prosecution's witnesses.

Our first night at the hotel was tranquil and comfortable. The hotel had colonial style décor. It had portraits of our nation's founding fathers hanging on the walls. It made me think about my American History class in grade school. It looked and felt like Fort Knox, because there were Alcohol, Tobacco, Firearms, and Explosives (ATF) agents everywhere. There were men and women with guns, ready to use them. We were assigned our own agent to escort us. I later found out that after our testimony we would move to another hotel, the Holiday Inn-Isle of Capri, where family members of victims were staying.

The next morning I awoke to the ringing of our room telephone. It was Attorney Conrad. He informed me that we had to meet with the lead prosecutor, his boss, Attorney Paul Ebert. They wanted to brief us of what we could expect during questioning. He wasn't sure exactly when we would be taken to the court house for testimony. Things were starting to get serious. My emotions ran so rampant, I went numb. I couldn't feel anything. My Post-traumatic stress disorder was in full affect. This was definitely going to be a defining moment in my life, and the life of my daughter Tamara. We were going face to face with John Allen Muhammad. We were going to be within a few feet of a man that came to our home to murder me and who murdered innocent Keenya.

The thing that really concerned us the most was that he was going to have to face us. Would we be adequately protected? John Muhammad hated me enough to send a boy to my door to kill me. I watched too many movies when the defendant grabbed some officer's weapon and shot up the entire court room. Would he be remorseful? Would he be angry that I was alive and try to intimidate me as a witness? Would I snap and jump over the witness stand, jump across the table, and put my hands around his deranged neck and squeeze every ounce of breath out of him? All of these questions ran through my mind.

The next morning Tamara and I woke up to prepare for who knows what. We prayed together in our room. I was still numb, I could imagine how my child was feeling. We got dressed and went downstairs for breakfast. We both sat there looking at the food. Our stomachs were not having any food. We decided to go to the task force room in the hotel and wait for our ride to the court house. The ATF task force was busy, but not too busy to offer us their condolences. They were so kind and compassionate toward all of us. As for me, I had not felt this feeling before. My experience in Tacoma with our law enforcement was rigid and adversarial, to say the least. These people in Virginia were genuinely interested in me and my daughter. They took the time to include me in their work. Whatever they were working on, it was no big concealment. I asked questions regarding information that I saw on their tactical boards. They answered my questions. There was no conspiracy or secrets. For the first time since Keenya's murder investigation, I felt included. There were some answers to my questions. I saw names and locations that I recognized, like Mildred Muhammad, Robert Holmes, Bellingham, and Tacoma.

Someone said "Mrs. Nichols, Mrs. Isa Nichols and Tamara Nichols." It was time to go to the courthouse. Tamara and I were escorted to the lobby. When we arrived, there were several men standing around. They were officers of the Tacoma Police Department, Tacoma Fire Department, the forensics unit and the coroner. The timid looking black man that was smoking cigarettes, one after the other, was also there. I looked at him and smiled. I smiled because he seemed so nervous and fearful. I was nervous, but not fearful. We were escorted to different vans and surrounded by ATF personnel and undercover officers. We were heavily guarded. Every last one of them had a weapon. The ATF personnel were always courteous, but very official.

When we arrived, we were given explicit instructions to avoid the media. The media was everywhere. They could only come within a few feet of us, as there were barricades blocking them. We were told that we had to go through security and be searched before entering the courthouse building. Our entrance to the courthouse was not the main entrance. We had to walk through long corridors and many doors. I held my daughter's hand, we were both being brave. It was Tamara and I that saw Keenya's murder at our home. No one else in the Nichols' family saw that devastation. Those images will forever be in our mind's consciousness. Now, here we were together as key witnesses in the trial of the century.

Upon arriving to the courtroom we were greeted by Attorney Conrad. He asked Tamara and me to follow him to a room near the courtroom. He told us that the jury had reached a verdict in John's murder case, and we had to wait to meet Attorney Paul Ebert. There was so much activity. People and the media were rapidly entering the courtroom. Those of us that had just arrived had to wait in a room. Law enforcement officers were walking around with their hands on their gun holsters. There was silence all around. We were told to be patient and quiet.

It was about twenty minutes, but it seemed like an hour. Suddenly the courtroom door opened and a man ran out and shouted "Guilty!"

He was guilty on all counts! After six hours over two days, the jury had convicted him on two counts of capital murder. People were pouring out of the courtroom in tears. I moved closer so I could see. They were holding their faces in their hands. Some were walking right past me. Many were holding one another up. I could only stand there and look at the emotions of the different people walking out of the courtroom.

My eyes caught the eyes of a beautiful, petite tearful, Korean woman. She was crying as she walked toward me. As I stared, my arms left my side and extended toward her. She walked right into them. I held her as she cried and she held on to me. Who was this women? I had no idea. Whoever she was, my spirit connected with hers at that very moment.

I found out later that she was the sister of Hong Im Ballenger of Louisiana. Hong was leaving work at a beauty supply store when she was struck in the head by a Bushmaster rifle bullet.

I could hardly walk. Never in my life could I imagine such tragedy in America. I had not felt this remorseful since the 9-11 attacks, which wasn't so long ago. I saw people coming out of the courtroom that day that meant something to me. I was one of them. I was a family member of John and Lee's first murder victim. Up until that day, I was isolated. It was almost as if her 21-year-old life had no importance. Keenya was just an unsolved murder in Tacoma. Up until that day, Keenya's death was not even known to any of these hurting people. Their murders were so close to each other and so many that all the focus was on the East Coast.

However, there was a murder that precipitated all the murders, at my front door. It was an incredible day. I felt that my life was finally on the road to some type of recovery, from a time of isolation and loneliness. For eight months I had no one to really share my true feelings, fears, and frustrations. I kept so much inside. In counseling, I would talk to my therapist at The Healing Circle. The sessions were never enough time to get my feelings out. One hour was just not enough time for me. I didn't get a chance to touch the surface of my pain.

Attorney Conrad approached me and said that Attorney Ebert was ready to see me. Tamara and I followed him to a nearby room. Mr. Ebert entered and we shook hands and sat down. He said that they had just finished John's trial. We were going to begin the penalty phase, then the sentencing. Now that they had gotten a guilty verdict, the next step was to present evidence to convince the jury that John Muhammad deserved to die. The jury had only two options to consider in the penalty phase of the trial; the death sentence or life in prison. Attorney Paul Ebert was going for the death penalty.

They explained to Tamara and I that we were going to be sworn in, then asked some questions about the events of Keenya's murder. They wanted to make sure that we were prepared to see pictures take by the coroner of Keenya. The pictures would be graphic, showing the bullet entry into Keenya's face. They wanted us to just tell what happened to us on that day. We needed to give details.

There were other witnesses that they were going to call that day. One of them was Mildred Muhammad. I had not seen or spoken with Mildred since our conversation on whether I should write a book about my life. I missed my friend. I did not let the attorney know that we had been estranged. Attorney Conrad seemed pleased that we would see each other again. His understanding was that we were close. He said she was arriving that evening. I asked if I could see her. He said that I could as long as we didn't discuss the case. He was going to let her know that I wanted to see her. I couldn't help but wonder if she missed me, if she would want to see me.

Since the jury's verdict had come in, Judge Millette ordered that we start the penalty phase of the trial the next morning at 9 a.m. They took all the Tacoma witnesses back to the hotel. Tamara and I went to the hotel restaurant for dinner. Tamara, my baby girl, had been with me all the while. She was the reason for me to remain sane. I had to fight for us. I had made up my mind that I was not going to let her life go nowhere, but upward and out of our horror. She and I had been at an emotional bottom for so long. I had to love her back to me, back to herself, back to God. I looked into her eyes sitting across the table. She was incredible. She was strong, vulnerable, and volatile at the same time. I told her that we were there to bring closure for Keenya, to see justice for Keenya.

I received a call on my cell phone. It was Mildred. Attorney Conrad had given her my cell number. She had arrived at the hotel. I gave her my room number and we arranged to get together that evening after she checked in and was settled in her room. When we left the restaurant, we actually ran into

Mildred in the lobby. She was with a Caucasian woman. I approached them both. Mildred looked at me and smiled. We hugged. She introduced the woman to me as her attorney. I said hello and immediately focused on my friend. I asked how her children were? Before she could respond we were interrupted by her attorney. Their room was ready and she was tired. Mildred took her room key from her. She told me that she would call me later. I didn't talk with her anymore that evening or the next day.

At about 7 a.m. the telephoned rang, startling me. It was the task force telling me that Tamara and I would be testifying and we needed to be at the courthouse at 9 a.m. The shuttle was leaving at 8:15 a.m. It would be just a few hours before Tamara and I would be in a courtroom, sitting within a few feet of John Allen Williams, a.k.a. John Allen Muhammad. John Muhammad, a black man that had turned into a coward; a sick, diabolical, human being. A black man that feels that I cost him his marriage, his business, and his children. I was responsible for all his problems. The price he wanted me to pay was my life. Any life would do.

When we arrived to the courthouse we were searched, given badges and taken to the courtroom. There were the same Tacoma professionals that responded to the crime scene. There were a couple of younger white males. I had not seen them before. There again was the tall, skinny, dark-skinned black man smoking cigarette after cigarette. Next to the courtroom was a waiting room. Tamara and I stayed in the waiting room until it was time for us to be called to the witness stand. We heard some of the names from the people in our Tacoma group. They entered the courtroom. We were not able to hear any testimony. We could not go into the court until after we had testified and the judge dismissed us as witnesses. Once we were dismissed as witnesses, we could attend the rest of the trial. I had traveled across the country, of course I was going to sit in John's trial. There were so much that I needed to know. The answers to my many questions were in that courtroom. It was Tacoma's time to be heard.

A sheriff's deputy from the courtroom came into the waiting room where I was sitting. He said, "Mrs. Isa Nichols, please take the stand." I stood up and slowly followed the deputy into the court room. There were deputies standing everywhere with their hands on their guns. John was sitting behind a table, beside his attorneys, facing the judge. I walked right past him. I went to the witness stand and put my hand on the Bible. I swore to tell the truth. I was asked to be seated.

Isa Nichols points out Muhammad during the penalty phase of the convicted sniper's trial.
AP Photo

People were staring at me. I wore a silk, fuchsia-colored, two-piece suit. I wore that suit to be bright and colorful. I wanted John to remember me that day. I wanted him to see that I was still here, alive. The devil took his best shot to kill, steal, and destroy my life, but I was there for John to see that Jesus saves. I took one look at John. I was breathless. I willed myself to breathe. It was him. He took a quick glance up at me and I looked him in his eyes. He then looked down at a tablet and doodled. He looked so cold and distant. There was no longer any resonance of a loving husband, father, or human being. John had lost his sound mind, unable to love ever again. He appeared as if nothing happened.

Looking at John, I wondered in my mind why he would commit so many murders. It was what everyone wanted to know. Up until I appeared there, John and Lee were just a pair of vagabonds that showed up on the East Coast. Here I was, attending the trial for the murderer of Dean Harold Meyers; while in another courtroom, in a different county, was the trial for the murderer of Linda Franklin.

I sat beside the Meyer family during the trial. They heard every testimony, seen every piece of evidence that the State of Virginia had proving that John Allen Muhammad mercilessly shot their brother while he pumped gas at a local station. The Meyer family were the nicest people you could meet. They consoled me while in the midst of all their pain. They had sat in the court room for many months attending the trial. Listening to many horrid details of how their beloved brother was brutally killed. They invited Tamara and me to have dinner with them. I knew that they wanted to know more about me. They wanted to know about Keenya. I wanted to tell them. I was ready to share. What I had to say, they needed to hear. Keenya was now included in the chronology of victims, of loved ones that were murdered.

During the course of a week, I met and dined with many family members of the victims, including Denise Johnson, the wife of Conrad Johnson, who was the last victim before John and Lee were captured. Her husband was shot on his bus route. She was now a widow with two children to raise without their father. Denise Johnson's acquaintance was unique to me, Conrad's murder was last while Keenya's murder was first. I was the Alpha and she was the Omega, the beginning and the end. Here was a beautiful sister that I had come to admire. She was gentle, yet she was strong. She missed her husband very much, she never imagined she would be living her life without him.

One evening, I was invited to attend a birthday dinner for Linda Buchanan. Linda was the sister of Sunny Buchanan, who was murdered while mowing his lawn. Linda's mother had invited all of the family members of victims to come and celebrate Linda. I managed to pick up some cheer, and so did others, because when I arrived everyone was there enjoying themselves. We looked like a United Nations convention. The colors of our skin represented many cultures. These murders were random and penetrated the diversity of what families in this country look like. I thought about a song I learned in the children's choir at church; *Jesus loves the little children, all the children of the world. Red, yellow, black, and white; they are precious in his sight. Jesus loves the little children of the world.*

This mental video will play in my mind forever. This was an impact on my life that I would never forget. Two years had gone by since the tragedy at my home. Family members were given an opportunity to tell Judge Millette about our feelings. The judge would read them before rendering the penalty for the crime. I completed an impact statement. I wrote:

February 16, 2004

Honorable Judge LeRoy Millette Jr. C/O
Victim Witness Assistance Program
Office of the Commonwealth's Attorney
9401 Grant Avenue
Manassas, VA 20110

RE: Impact of Defendant John Allen Muhammad's
*   Murder of Keenya Cook*
*   February 16, 2002*

Dear Sir;
I want to take this opportunity to thank the Commonwealth of Virginia for their support, professionalism, genuine compassion, and advocacy for Tamara Nichols and myself during the trial. We were indeed blessed to have met the many family members of victims during our stay in Virginia. We have been so isolated in Washington State, as most of the focus was on the murder crimes in Washington D.C. and neighboring communities.

It was in Virginia when advocacy and understanding of my loss was finally realized. The impact stems in a horrid array of lies, deception, conspiracy, and a merciless killing. Keenya's murder is no longer a mystery, or a rumor of just another black on black crime. I was a suspect along with other family members. Detectives accused me of having an affair with another man. (Talk about defamation of character!) My husband was accused of having an affair with another woman. The detectives told me that an insurance policy had been taken out on my life. (Apparently they were just probing.) My innocent, 3.68 GPA receiving daughter was accused of being connected with a gang. Until October 26, 2002, Keenya's horrifying murder was an unsolved murder. On October 26, 2002, Tacoma saw John Muhammad on their TV screens. It was at that point Keenya's killer was tied to John Muhammad and Lee Malvo; commonly known as the D.C. snipers.

It was in Virginia when the world came to know this case as one of the worst cases of domestic violence in the history of this country. It was in Virginia that what was known about last to the world, was actually the first murder committed. That Tacoma, Washington was the training ground for a mass murderer. That John Allen Muhammad's depravity of mind began BEFORE he lost his children in a custody hearing to his ex-wife, Mildred. That he had turned his friends into accomplices that aided and abetted his warped thinking and vindictiveness.

Keenya Cook was my beautiful, intelligent, witty, resourceful, 21-year-old niece. She was the youngest of three children born to my sister-in-law Pamela Nichols. Keenya was a wonderful mother at the time to a six-month-old daughter, Angeleah Rogers (Angel). Angeleah is now 2 years of age. Keenya and Angel had moved into our home with my husband Joseph (Keenya's uncle), daughter Tamara, and I, in October of 2001. She asked her uncle and I if she could stay, as she no longer wanted to live with, Angel's father. He had beaten Keenya on several occasions and Keenya was afraid for her and daughter Angeleah. He was abusive, violent, and a drug abuser during their relationship.

Keenya, Joseph, and I sat down with Keenya and discussed some of the goals Keenya wanted for her and the baby. Joseph and I felt her goals were realistic and obtainable. Her goals were to become safe and heal from abuse, get employment, save her money, move into an apartment with Angeleah. She had applied for the Section 8 Housing Assistance Grant, and was on the waiting list. Everyday Keenya took care of Angeleah, looked for employment, and looked into enrolling in vocational schools for training. As with any extended family member, we enjoyed Keenya, appreciated her, and loved her very much.

Keenya had been in our home for three months. It was Valentine's Day; Keenya had left with the baby to go and visit with Angelo on Wednesday 2/14/03. She and Angeleah returned back home on Saturday 2/16/02 around 2:30 pm. Keenya was in a terrific mood. She had a positive weekend. She returned with a Valentine's Day balloon, a rose that she received from Angelo. Around 3:30 pm Keenya, Angeleah, and I went to the Safeway Grocery Store to shop for food. Angel was a beautiful baby girl, and we could hardly go a few feet without someone stopping to notice her. We had taken two hours, as we liked to watch Angel's expressions and reactions in the store.

Keenya and I returned home at around 5 p.m. or so. Keenya had taken the baby and placed her in a walker, while we put up the groceries. Keenya had asked if I would fix some chicken tacos for dinner. I told her I would; however we noticed that we did not have any tortilla shells for the meal. Around 6:30 pm or so, I left to pick up my daughter Tamara from a friend's house and go back to the store. I asked Keenya to boil the chicken breast meat in some water. Tamara and I returned around 7:30 pm or so. Tamara went into the house to open the garage door for me.

Tamara returned to the car, looking horrified. She came to tell me that Keenya was lying in the doorway, and that the house was smokey. I went to the door, and there Keenya lay. Her feet were in the doorway. Her head was near the stairway. I thought she must have succumbed to smoke inhalation. I turned off the burning pot on the stove in the kitchen. When I returned to Keenya, her eyes were open and fixed, her hands were stiff and cold. There, next to her head, was a pool of blood. Along side of her head was a piece of metal. I jumped up to find baby Angel. The baby was upstairs asleep, lying on the bed naked. Next to Angel was a diaper, pajamas, a bottle of milk, and baby lotion; Keenya had just given her a bath. I was horrified and manic. I wasn't sure if the baby was injured. When I touched her, she awoke screaming and crying. I took her downstairs, handed her to Tamara, and told them to go to our neighbor's house. Tamara was stoic, she had went into shock. I had to repeat over and over to her my instructions to go to the neighbor's house. I called paramedics; they arrived and could not resuscitate Keenya. She was dead. She had been shot, point-blank in the face.

The impact of Keenya's murder by John and Lee is perpetual for me at this time. It was just Tamara and myself that day that saw the devastation, the tragic murder scene of Keenya. Tamara, who had just turned 14 years old on 2/4/2002, is now 16. She has been diagnosed with post-traumatic stress disorder and depression. Her entire life of safety, being secure, and confident, and the security of living in her own home, no longer exist. My once normal teenager is now traumatized. Since that day, she has been on a downward spiral of emotion fear, rage, and grief. She had been listening to family members share their thoughts, pain, and accusations. She began to resent me and blame me for Keenya's death. She felt that if I had not been in 'anyone else's business her cousin would be alive'. She has re-occurring nightmares of being shot in the face. She has many sleepless nights. Tamara has experimented with drugs, and almost overdosed twice. She just wanted to disassociate with the pain. Tamara is receiving therapy, and is on anti-depressant/anxiety medication.

Her emotions are so volatile that her GPA went from a 3.86 down to a 2.33. I had to change her to a new school due to the notoriety of the murder. Tamara is on a Special 504 Accommodation Plan, which allows students with physical and emotional challenges, special assistance and support through school and even into college. I will continue to love Tamara through this, and provide what ever support that I can. GOD will heal my daughter's wounds and scars. There is purpose and a destiny for her life.

I had no idea that John and Mildred were estranged at the time, until that day of my visit. When I stopped by to pay a visit to Mildred, John, and the children, I had no idea the impact would be so tragic or that it would ever lead to me or one of my family members being murdered. The impact stems from a decision that I made in the year 2000 to help Mildred Muhammad find refuge in a shelter, medical attention, and support from law enforcement. To help her with the devastation of having her three small children taken out of school, and within hours taken to Antiqua without a trace. I had no idea that John Muhammad was in the depraved mindset that he had succumbed to.

I did what any true friend would do for someone that they cared about. I cared about the Muhammad family as a whole. Today, I live with the impact of the end of a twenty-year marriage, the loss of a beloved niece, and the loss of a family of in-laws that I love so much, helped, and provided food and shelter. I have recurring dreams of the murder scene of my home. I live with the blame for my husband's feelings of guilt for not providing the safety that he promised his niece. My husband Joseph and his family members are angry that his wife was responsible for John Muhammad's retaliation against his family.

I have to live with the pain that my decision to help Mildred caused John Muhammad to send Lee Malvo to the front door of my home, with an earphone in his ear, taking orders to shoot unsuspecting Keenya point blank in her face, while sixth-month-old Angeleah laid for hours upstairs waiting for her mama to return. I have to live with the pain of not knowing who could do such a thing, to have no regard for another human life, while John and Lee went back to their accomplice and friend's home. Knowing how they hung around Tacoma, Washington as chameleons, watching the breaking news story for weeks of the mysterious death of 21-year-old Keenya

Cook. The impact on Keenya's infant daughter, not growing up with her mother, is now having to grow up with the assistance of the State to aid in taking care of her. I now live with impacts of economical dysfunction that are a result of my extensive treatments for major depression, sleep depravation, and anxiety. Impacts that have caused financial devastation to me, while others are making profit from movies, writing books, etc., as families of victims like myself have been too unstable to face the public, work at their jobs and businesses.

Keenya's murder case in Tacoma, Washington is still open. While the impact of John and Lee's trials may have brought closure to many victim murders, it brought out vital and critical information for me. Unlike the random sniper victims, Keenya's murder was pre-meditated. The evidence is more than circumstantial in her case. John planned it as retaliation for my choosing to help Mildred find her children. It was their first mission to kill, with Mildred being their last kill. (Thank GOD they were caught within a few miles of Mildred's Maryland home.)

I now live with the impact of the question of whether or not Tacoma police authorities are trying to cover-up some major mistakes that apparently occurred on their parts when Mildred was seeking assistance in the very beginning. Mildred had given several statements and reports, warning local and federal authorities of the violent and dangerous change in her husband. It was her filings of anti-harassment documents that prevented John from being able to legally purchase guns. I had provided information to Tacoma detectives on every occasion that John contacted me by telephone from Washington, Canada, and Antiqua looking for Mildred. After they were found in 2001 and the judge ruled that the children be turned over to Mildred, John never contacted me again looking for Mildred.

I offer my victim impact statement in hope that the understanding and the extent of John Allen Muhammad and Lee Boyd Malvo's killings deserve the recommended punishment for the crimes committed. I'm grateful to Prince William County Commonwealth Attorney Paul Ebert for presenting a well-structured case for the senseless and brutal murder of Dean Harold Meyers. I appreciate the integrity and professionalism extended to all the family members of the many victims, including Mildred Muhammad and her three children, for they are truly a family that is victimized. John Muhammad's depravity of mind began many years before the divorce from his wife and abduction of his three children.

The inclusion of other family member victims in the Dean Harold Meyers' trial allowed for much needed support. It allowed me to look John Allen Muhammad in the face and make my peace, so that true forgiveness could begin to come in and heal my hurt; thus confirming that "no weapon formed against me shall prosper." It fostered a very diverse group of people to come together from all over the United States to strengthen and console one another. My presence was received with much compassion and I had a chance to support others who shared similar pains. I commend the jury on their due diligence to daily sift through the horrid details, and find what was needed for them to render their decision; a decision that would bring closure and vindication to many hurting family members.

It is my hope that as judge, you will do what is necessary to ensure that John Allen Muhammad does not hurt anyone else. That as judge, you will set the precedent that the laws of our country will be adhered to and criminals are punished to the fullest extent of the law. That as judge, you would order some level of compensation of restitution for Keenya Cook's now two-year-old daughter, Angeleah Rogers, and other victim families who have suffered as a result of John's crimes.

Respectfully,

Isa Nichols

From Pain to Purpose

There comes a time when you have to take your pain and turn it into power. Until today, I was afraid that I would never get my life back together. My daughter Tamara is in her first year of college in Tennessee. My oldest daughter finished college at Saint Augustine's College in North Carolina, married a wonderful young man, and gave birth to twin baby girls. I am the proud grandmother to twin baby girls. I saw their births. I was alive. I was alive and living. I was alive to see my family grow. I was alive to see my father look at and hold his great grandchildren.

I have sold my home in Tacoma. I lived there for four years while behind in my mortgage payments. For four years, I was unstable and unable to work. My depression affected me physically. I owed $65,000 in mortgage payments. Yes! God took good care of me when I couldn't take care of myself.

I am waiting for my final divorce decree from my husband of twenty-two years. It was time to let go. For years I didn't have the courage. I believe God can do any and everything. God spoke to my heart. He said that my marriage covenant was made to Him in front of witnesses, not to witnesses. I kept my covenant to Him. I was His daughter. He fearfully and wonderfully created me for His purpose, to do great and marvelous things on the earth. He has already prepared a table before me in the presence of my enemies. Goodness and mercy was with me all along. He was making me the head and not the tail.

God is love. His love lives inside of me. I am in a new season. Love has brought me back! I have renewed my strength and I am mounting up like an eagle. Sometimes it is a struggle, but I take everyday one day at a time. I take care of myself and I am comfortable with just me. Love flows through me. I have found new roads to travel on. If I come to a block in the road, I can choose to move the block or make another road. I have much work to do.

The Gift Of Forgiveness

I made up my mind that although my internal wounds may be deep, forgiveness heals the wounds. Forgiveness is vital to healing. I started forgiveness in two Virginia courtrooms. I looked John Allen Muhammad in his face and I prayed that Jesus Christ, son of God, would have mercy on his soul. I attended the trial of Lee Boyd Malvo. I was able to see the face of the youth that was sent to my front door by John to kill me. He killed Keenya as proof he could follow orders from John. I prayed that Jesus Christ, the son of God, would have mercy on his soul. God had mercy for Adam and Eve after their sin. I know that the God I serve desired to heal, and delivered the two that were created; He desires a relationship with them. I prayed for their families. I made my peace with them both. It was necessary for my life. Today I have a changed attitude. I have an attitude of gratitude. I am grateful to be alive.

I have put forgiveness in the forefront each day. I also asked to be forgiven. After Keenya's murder, I apologized to many people. I spent an entire year apologizing. I apologized for Keenya's death occurring in my home. I apologized for the pain that everyone had. I apologized for John and Lee not killing me. I apologized because the Nichols' family needed to hear me say it. I apologized to them at a news conference on national TV. I apologized so people that resent me can either accept the apology or move on with their lives.

Apologies can have an impact or not. I know people who abuse their spouses and apologize shortly thereafter, or until the next abusive occurrence. If more people would apologize when they become aware of an offense, relationships would flourish. In some of my most difficult times in my marriage, receiving a simple sincere apology could have put us on the road to healing, greater love, and commitment. Some people have problems with apologizing, even when they know that they are wrong. They associated it as admission of guilt or weakness in some way. There are apologies that have no sincerity. I make it a point to be sincere. There must be a change in my mind about how I feel about my offense, or else I won't give one.

There are areas in my life that are still in healing. Deep wounds have to heal from the inside outward. The analogy of a scab comes to mind. When I was child, I was a tomboy. In being rough with the neighborhood guys, I would encounter some accidents. I was always skinning up my knee caps. I would injure myself on my skates or bicycle. Sometimes, the wound would go beyond the surface and be under the skin into my flesh. The trauma to that knee would hurt badly in the beginning. It even hurt to put medication on it to disinfect it. The next couple of days, I could hardly move the leg. If I bent the knee, the wound would throb. I had to keep the knee still. Slowly, the healing would occur. A scab would cover the opening. The scab covered the injured area, until I picked it. If I picked it too soon, it would bleed and be delayed in healing. The scab would get smaller, and eventually fall off. My sore was no longer in any danger. I could go on to my regular activities.

My emotional wounds are the same way. They are deep and must take some time to heal. Healed, delivered, and set free to minister is my ultimate goal. I have picked at the wound by sometimes going into unhealthy environments, being with people that don't genuinely care for or love me. That always hurt. It was re-hurting the hurt. Just as it takes time to heal a deep sore, it takes time to heal deep emotional scars. You have to pamper your emotional wound. You risk letting it get infected if you don't. I don't allow any room for reinfection. You can't pick at it or it will cause more pain. The powerful thing is that it does heal. Psalm 91 is my promise of security. In verses 14-16, God says, "Those who love me, I will deliver; I will protect those who know my name. When they call to me, I will answer them, I will be with them in trouble, I will rescue them and honor them. With long life I will satisfy them, and show them my salvation."

As a survivor of satan's assignment to send John Muhammad and Lee Malvo to my door to kill me, I testify wholeheartedly to Matthew 5:44, "But I say unto you, Love your enemies, bless them that curse you, do good to them that hate you, and pray for them which despitefully use you, and persecute you." This also requires dying. Almost daily! You must die inside yourself and let the love of Christ with His blood resurrect you in everyway! Only then can you receive the gift of forgiveness to continue to love, bless, and do good.

The dissolution of a 22 year marriage is a great loss. I did not enter into marriage with the intentions of it ever ending. There is a grieving process. A part of me actually died. Through a process of self-discovery, I have found the Genesis of a virtuous woman. I will continue to be a woman that continues to put God first and will be a jewel in any man's crown. My pain has now empowered me to be an agent for change. I speak a language of truth and reconciliation. I use a vocabulary that says restoration and redemption. The purpose for the pain is now clear to me.

Jireh-Shalom Foundation – A New Vision

My future is whatever God has for me. He is not finished with me. I am another epistle of a testimony. I will tell a remarkable story of God's love that transcended above hate, anger, and abandonment, into love, restoration, and reconciliation. I have more purpose to help children, families, and our communities with ***InPowerMent*** through transformation, and renewing of their minds. As a believer in the Trinity, and as a survivor, I embrace the challenge.

Something of value must come from the trail of tears and shattered lives. Jireh-Shalom Foundation is that something. Jireh-Shalom are Hebrew words meaning provision and peace. The need for provision and peace for abused women, and abused women with children, is an overwhelming phenomenon. Through a collaborative approach and a philosophy of unconditional acceptance, Jireh-Shalom Foundation offers the opportunity for truth and reconciliation, and for the disenfranchised to receive forgiveness, help, hope, and guidance. The Jireh-Shalom model is a transformative process that transforms domestic abuse sufferers through a process of truth and reconciliation in their lives. This transformation is a result of their self-discovery. This is my passion. This is my legacy to domestic abuse and domestic violence survivors like me. This may be the last thing I do for healing, education, and domestic ***InPowerMent*** of our children, our families, and our community.

Well, I thought it was the last thing I do for healing. On January 1, 2008 Lee Boyd Malvo called my cell phone. It was New Year's Day. I was in the kitchen preparing ham, greens, yams, black eyed peas, macaroni and cheese, cornbread, gumbo etc., when I answered the phone. "Hello this is Lee." His accent was strong, and his voice was sensitive. I asked, Lee who? "Lee Malvo, DC Sniper." I was silent, I didn't know what to say or do? I finally asked why he was calling. There was silence. I didn't say anything, he didn't say anything. I said yes, I forgive you. He hung up.

My heart was beating so fast, I had to sit down. I checked the internet to make sure nothing crazy like an escape had occurred. I paced back and forth in the living room. I couldn't believe that I had spoken with him. Lee Malvo is now 21 years old. He is not the same 16 year old boy I saw in the Virginia court room. I had forgiven him the first time as a child, now he was a man. I had heard once that he had contacted sniper victim Linda Franklin's daughter on her cell phone. She was so traumatized that they called for help. However for me, I felt compelled to forgive him. It was an interesting first day in the 2008 New Year all around. My former husband was coming over to have dinner with Tamara, my father and me. We reached our truth, our reconciliation and had arrived at forgiveness. GOD IS ABLE!

Appendix

AP Photo

Convicted sniper John Allen Muhammad is escorted into Courtroom 10 at the Virginia Beach Circuit Court in Virginia Beach, Va., Nov. 24, 2003.

Conrad Johnson

The 35-year-old bus driver was shot October 22 in Silver Spring, Maryland. He was standing on the top step of his empty bus when he was hit. The father of two was a 10-year county employee, who "loved basketball, loved his kids," Montgomery County executive Doug Duncan said. Johnson, from nearby Oxon Hill, Maryland, was shot in the stomach, apparently as he was getting off the bus in a staging area for Montgomery County's Ride On commuter line.

Unidentified man

A 37-year-old man from Melbourne, Florida, was shot and wounded at about 8 p.m. EDT on October 19 as he and his wife were leaving a Ponderosa restaurant in Ashland, Virginia, near Richmond. The couple were traveling through the state. The bullet pierced the man's upper abdomen and tore through several organs. Surgeons removed part of the stomach, the left half of the pancreas and the entire spleen. His surgeon, Dr. Rao Ivatury, said the victim, who is 6 feet tall and weighs 200 pounds, "is a very, very strong man, and once he comes out of this I think he'll have a normal life. But it's going to be a bumpy road, a long process." The victim's wife issued a statement, thanking the people of Richmond for their support and prayers for her husband. She also asked people to "pray also for the attacker and that no one else is hurt."

Linda Franklin

Linda Franklin, 47, an FBI analyst, had just finished shopping at a Home Depot in Falls Church, Virginia, when she was killed October 14. Police said the Arlington, Virginia, woman was with her husband when she was shot once as she loaded items in her car in a Seven Corners Shopping Center parking garage, around 9:15 p.m. ET. Sources said Franklin worked for the FBI's National Infrastructure Protection Center and said there was no indication she was targeted because of her occupation. (Service for victim)

Johnson and Franklin
AP Photo

Kenneth Bridges

Kenneth Bridges, 53, a Philadelphia, Pennsylvania, businessman, was killed as he filled his gas tank at an Exxon station off I-95 near Fredericksburg, Virginia, the morning of October 11. The co-founder of a marketing distribution company, Bridges was in the area on a business trip. A friend, Gary Shepherd, said the family was "shocked and saddened by this senseless event." "Ken was a loving husband, father of six children and an outstanding citizen of the Philadelphia community," Shepherd said. "While no family should have to endure this type of tragedy, the Bridges family hopes that this killer is brought to justice as quickly as possible."

Bridges and Meyers
AP Photo

Dean Harold Meyers

On October 9, Dean Harold Meyers, 53, was fatally shot as he pumped gas at a station in Manassas, Virginia. Meyers was a civil engineer from Gaithersburg, Maryland, and a Vietnam War veteran.

Woman, boy

On October 4, a 43-year-old woman was shot and critically injured in a Fredericksburg, Virginia, parking lot. She later was released from the hospital. She was not identified. The sniper's eighth victim was a 13-year-old boy who was shot in the abdomen October 7 after his aunt dropped him off at a middle school in Maryland's Prince George's County. His aunt, a nurse, rushed him to a hospital in Bowie. He was airlifted to a Washington hospital, where doctors removed his spleen and parts of his stomach and pancreas. He remains in critical but stable condition.

Pascal Charlot

Pascal Charlot, 72, who was killed the evening of October 3 on a Washington street, was the only sniper victim killed in the nation's capital.

A retired carpenter, Charlot immigrated to the United States from Haiti. He is survived by his wife.

Rivera and Charlot
AP Photo

Lori Ann Lewis-Rivera

Lori Ann Lewis-Rivera was getting ready to vacuum out her van at a Kensington, Maryland, gas station when she was killed October 3. She grew up in a small town in Idaho and had recently moved east with her husband and daughter of preschool age. She was 25. "I mean, she comes and goes, and all of a sudden she gets caught up in this. It's just devastating," said neighbor Rosa Malon. "There are no words for it."

Sarah Ramos

Sarah Ramos also died the morning of October 3. Ramos, 34, was sitting on a bench reading outside a post office near a Silver Spring, Maryland, retirement community when she was shot in the head and killed. A native of El Salvador, Ramos was a member of several church groups and babysat for children and worked as a housekeeper. "The thing that impressed me about Sarah," said her employer, Larry Gaffigan, "when she walked into the room, not just a person walked in the room but something walked in the room with her. Something that just warmed the house and your soul." Ramos was married and had a 7-year-old son.

Walekar amd Ramos
AP Photo

Prem Kumar Walekar

Also on October 3, Prem Kumar Walekar, 54, was shot and killed while filling his minivan with gas at a service station in Aspen Hill, Maryland. It was his 25th wedding anniversary. "I just want everybody to know that my dad was ... the greatest person I ever met," said Walekar's son, Andrew. "I'm glad he was my father." Ordinarily, the part-time cabdriver from Olney, Maryland, would not have been at the gas station at that time of day, but he was trying to finish his runs early so he could enjoy the warm afternoon. Walekar was born in India and had intended to retire there.

James Buchanan

James "Sonny" Buchanan was known as a man with a big heart who was always ready to help others. The 39-year-old son of a retired Montgomery County, Maryland, police officer was an active

Martin and Buchanan
AP Photo

volunteer at the local Boys and Girls Club. He was an amateur poet and taught children how to garden.

"Sonny was the dad to literally 400 kids," said Gregory Wims, a friend and fellow volunteer at the club. "He came to the club two or three times a week, helped with homework, etc."

Buchanan previously ran a landscaping company but had gotten out of the business. He was mowing the lawn of a former customer's car dealership near Rockville, Maryland, the morning of October 3, when he was shot in the chest and killed.

James D. Martin

James D. Martin, a program analyst at the National Oceanic and Atmospheric Administration, was standing in the parking lot of a Wheaton, Maryland, grocery store when he was killed October 2. He was there to buy groceries for his church.

The 55-year-old was an amateur genealogist and a Civil War buff. He is survived by his wife and an 11-year-old son.

References

National Domestic Violence Hotline
1 (800) 799-SAFE or 1 (800) 787-3224 (TDD)
National Sexual Violence Resource Center
1(877) 739-3895 (Toll Free) – (24 hr access to information, resources, and research regarding sexual assault)

Maxine Mimms Academies
1602 MLK Jr. Way
Tacoma, WA 98405
(253) 627-5506
www.maxinemimmsacademy.org

Victims Rights Foundation, Inc.
National Office
814 W Diamond Ave. Suite 200
Gaithersburg, MD 20878
Phone (301) 212-4141 Fax (301) 258-9345
Email: gwimms@victimsrightsfoundation.org
Website: www.victimsrightsfoundation.org

Jireh-Shalom Foundation
1602 Martin Luther King Jr. Way
Tacoma, WA 98405
 (253) 269-2868
Email: isanichols@jireh-shalom.org
Website: www.jireh-shalom.org

Kingdom Life Ministries International
Sister Nations
401 N. Oak Forest Rd
Goldsboro, NC 27534
(919) 778-9112
Email: info@sisternations.com
Website: www.sisternations.com

Pacific Christian Center Church
3211 112th Street East
Tacoma, WA 98446
(253) 536-0801
Email: churchpcc@aol.com
Website: www.pacificchristiancenter.org

Recommended Readings

The Holy Bible
Author: The Father, His Son, Holy Spirit

Guard Your Heart
Author: Dr. Kathy Shorter

The Power In You and *Take Control of Your Thoughts*
Author: Dr. Donald Shorter

Giving Birth To Me
Author: Dawn Kirkwood

Angel With A Broken Wing: My Journey Into Healing
Author: Valerie Yarborough

I Send My Blankets Over You: Lessons of Love: Poems, Stories and Songs for Healing, Transformation and Co-Creating New Realities
Author: Darya Funches. Ed.D

All The Joy You Can Stand: 101 Sacred Power Principles For Making Joy Real In Your Life
Author: Debrena Jackson Gandy